The Ultimate Beginners Guide to Wholesale Real Estate Investing

Real Estate Investing, Volume 6

Jim Pellerin

Published by Jim Pellerin, 2023.

THE ULTIMATE BEGINNERS GUIDE TO WHOLESALE REAL ESTATE INVESTING

First edition. April 27, 2023.

ISBN: 979-8223941019

Written by Jim Pellerin.

Also by Jim Pellerin

Real Estate Investing

Real Estate Investing Strategies: The Secret to Financial Independence with Real Estate

Real Estate Investing with Lease Options - Investing in Real Estate with No Money Down

Invest Now - The Passive Approach to Winning at Real Estate

The Ultimate Beginners Guide to Real Estate Investing

The 98 Best Real Estate Investing Strategies

The Ultimate Beginners Guide to Wholesale Real Estate Investing

Watch for more at www.jimpellerin.com.

Table of Contents

The Ultimate Beginners Guide to Wholesale Real Estate Investing

An Overiew of Wholesale

Real Estate Investing

Jim Pellerin

Updated for 2023

Why You Should Read This Book

Most people who want to get started with Real Estate Investing, have no idea how to get sarted. Or worse, they have some idea how to get started but it is the wrong strategy for them.

This book provides an overview of how to get started in Wholesale Real Estate Investing. This book is NOT a practical approach to Wholesale Real Estate Investing and the reader is NOT expected to be able to start wholesaling after completing this book.

In this book, you will learn enough information to be able to decide if wholesale real estate investing is right for you.

The Ultimate Beginners Guide to Wholesale Real Estate Investing

Real estate investing is easy. And **wholesale real estate investing** is the simplest real estate investing strategy to implement. But it also is the most time-consuming with the least reward. And it's the quickest way to make money in real estate if you are starting with no money.

House - Photo by Curtis Adams

There are only a few steps required to get started and be successful in wholesale real estate investing.

The biggest challenge with wholesale real estate investing is finding motivated sellers and properties for you to wholesale.

The key principles required to be successful in wholesale real estate investing are the amount of **time** you are willing to put into it and the amount of **persistence** you are willing to endure. You will also be faced with a lot of **rejection**, **criticism**, and not-so-pleasant **confrontations**.

The following chapters should give you enough information to get started and be successful in wholesale real estate investing. However, reading a book is never enough to be successful in any endeavor. Consider this book as an introduction to wholesale real estate investing.

For more information and additional free resources, be sure to check out my website at jimpellerin.com

Chapter 1: Introduction to Wholesale Real Estate Investing

Wholesale real estate investing is an attractive option for investors who want to enter the world of real estate without having to deal with the challenges of **owning** and **managing** properties.

Signing a Contract - Photo by Scott Graham

In this chapter, we will provide an overview of wholesale real estate investing and why it is a popular strategy among certain investors.

1.1 What is Wholesale Real Estate Investing?

Wholesale real estate investing is a real estate investment strategy that involves finding deeply discounted properties, putting those properties under contract, and assigning the contracts to other investors for a fee. Wholesalers do not own or manage the properties but rather act as **intermediaries** between sellers and buyers.

1.2 The process of wholesaling is simple

The process of wholesaling typically involves the following simple steps:

1. Finding a Motivated Seller and Property

The first step in wholesaling is finding a **motivated seller** who is willing to sell their property at a discounted price. This can be achieved through various means such as networking, direct mail campaigns, or even online advertising. Once a potential seller has been identified, the next step is to negotiate and sign a contract with them to purchase the property at a specific price.

2. Find a Buyer

After securing the contract, the wholesaler's next task is to market the property to **potential buyers**, typically other real estate investors, for a higher price. This can be done through various channels such as online listings, social media, or even word of mouth. The goal is to find a buyer who is willing to pay the contracted price and a fee, thus creating a profit for the wholesaler.

3. Assign the Contract

Once a buyer has been found, the wholesaler can **assign the contract** to them for a fee, typically known as an assignment fee. This fee is negotiated between the buyer and the wholesaler and is typically a percentage of the final sale price. The assignment fee is paid to the wholesaler by the buyer at closing.

The buyer also purchases the property from the seller at the contracted price that was negotiated by the wholesaler.

4. Receive Payment

Finally, the deal is closed, and the wholesaler **receives the assignment fee** from the buyer through the title company.

1.3 Pros and Cons of Wholesaling

There are several benefits to wholesaling, such as:

1. low financial risk,
2. minimal investment, and
3. quick turnaround times

However, there are also potential drawbacks, including the need for extensive market knowledge, the challenge of finding motivated sellers and buyers, and legal and ethical considerations.

1.4 Why Wholesaling is a Great Entry Point for Real Estate Investors

Wholesaling can be an ideal entry point for new investors who want to get started in real estate investing without the significant financial commitment and risks associated with owning and managing properties. Wholesaling allows investors to **gain experience** in negotiating deals, marketing properties, and building their network of buyers and sellers.

1.5 Setting Realistic Expectations for Wholesaling Success

While wholesaling can be a profitable and rewarding investment strategy, it is important to set realistic expectations for success. Wholesaling requires **hard work, dedication**, and the ability to adapt to changing market conditions. Wholesalers must also be prepared to navigate **legal and ethical considerations** when working with buyers and sellers.

1.6 Why wholesalers are important

Some critics suggest that wholesaling is an unethical strategy with the wholesaler ending up ripping off the seller. Nothing could be further from the truth.

Wholesalers play a crucial role in the real estate market as they provide a valuable service to both sellers and buyers. Sellers who are looking to get rid of their property quickly can benefit from the **convenience and speed** of working with a wholesaler, while buyers can take advantage of the **discounted prices** and potentially profitable investment opportunities.

Conclusion

In conclusion, wholesale real estate investing is an attractive investment strategy for investors looking to enter the real estate market without the challenges of owning and managing properties. This chapter has provided an introduction to wholesaling, including how it works, the pros and cons, and why it can be a great entry point for new investors. It is important for investors to set realistic expectations for success and be prepared to navigate the challenges of the wholesaling process.

Chapter 2: Creating a Long-Term Wholesaling Business Plan

Creating a long-term business plan is essential for any real estate wholesaler who wants to build a successful and sustainable business.

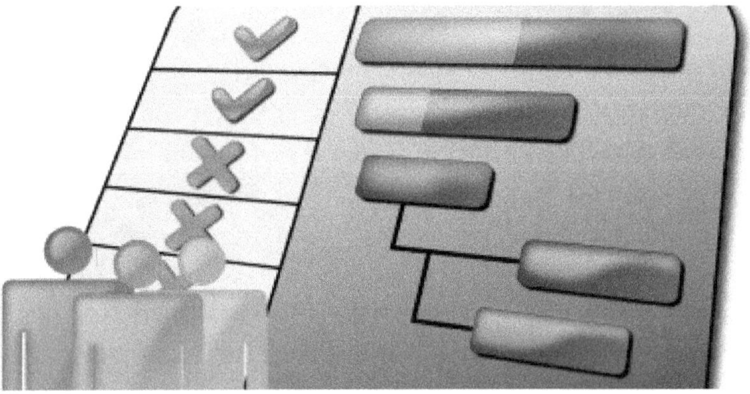

Plan - Photo by OpenClipart-Vectors

In this chapter, we will discuss the importance of setting long-term goals, developing a business plan, identifying your target market, refining your wholesaling processes, and continuously revising and updating your business plan.

2.1 Setting Long-Term Goals for Your Wholesaling Business

Setting long-term goals is essential for any business, and wholesale real estate investing is no exception. By setting **clear and specific goals**, you can create a **roadmap** for your business and measure your progress over time. Your goals might include the number of properties you want to wholesale in a year, the amount of revenue you want to generate, or the size of your buyer and seller network.

2.2 Developing a Business Plan to Achieve Your Goals

Once you have set your long-term goals, the next step is to develop a business plan that outlines the **strategies and tactics** you will use to achieve them.

Your business plan should include:

1. a detailed overview of your business,
2. your target market,
3. your marketing strategies,
4. your wholesaling processes, and
5. your financial projections

You should also identify potential **risks** and **challenges** that could impact your business and develop contingency plans to mitigate them.

2.3 Identifying Your Target Market and Marketing Strategies

To be successful in wholesale real estate investing, you need to have a clear understanding of your target market and develop effective marketing strategies to reach them. Your target market might include **distressed property owners**, **absentee owners**, and **buyers** who are looking to buy distressed properties. You should also develop a range of marketing strategies, such as **direct mail**, **online advertising**, and **networking events**, to reach potential buyers and sellers.

2.4 Evaluating Your Wholesaling Processes and Refining Your Approach

Once you have started wholesaling properties, it is important to **evaluate** your processes and **refine your approach** to improve your efficiency and profitability. You might consider automating certain tasks, such as lead generation or contract management, to save time and reduce the risk of errors. You should also review your processes **regularly** to identify areas for improvement and make adjustments to your strategy as needed.

2.5 Continuously Revising and Updating Your Business Plan

As your business evolves and your market changes, it is important to **continuously revise and update your business plan** to ensure that you stay on track to achieve your long-term goals. You might need to adjust your marketing strategies, refine your target market, or revise your financial projections based on changing market conditions.

Conclusion

In conclusion, creating a long-term business plan is essential for any real estate wholesaler who wants to build a successful and sustainable business. By setting clear goals, developing effective strategies, identifying your target market, refining your wholesaling processes, and continuously revising and updating your business plan, you can maximize your chances of success in the competitive world of wholesale real estate investing.

Chapter 3: Building Your Team

Wholesale real estate investing is a **team sport**, and building the right team is critical to your success.

Team - Photo by 089photoshootings

In this chapter, we will discuss the key players you need on your team, how to build relationships with real estate agents and brokers, and other wholesalers, how to collaborate with attorneys and accountants, and how to develop and nurture relationships with all key players.

3.1 Identifying Key Players in Your Wholesaling Business

To build a successful wholesaling business, you need to have the **right people on your team**. This includes a range of professionals such as real estate agents, attorneys, accountants, and other wholesalers. Each of these professionals plays a crucial role in your business, and it is important to identify the key players who can help you achieve your goals.

3.2 Building Relationships with Real Estate Agents and

Brokers

Real estate agents and brokers can be valuable partners in your wholesaling business. They can provide you with access to properties that are not listed on the market, help you to identify potential buyers, and assist you in negotiating deals. To build relationships with real estate agents and brokers, it is important to **network**, attend **industry events**, and provide value to them in any way you can.

3.3 Other Wholesalers

Acquisition wholesalers and **disposition** wholesalers can work together in a mutually beneficial way by collaborating on a process called **co-wholesaling** or **joint ventures**. Co-wholesaling is a partnership where acquisition wholesalers provide leads for potential real estate deals to disposition wholesalers, who then market and sell those properties to end buyers.

Acquisition wholesalers typically focus on finding distressed properties and negotiating favorable deals with sellers. Once they have secured the property, they may not have the resources, expertise, or desire to market and sell it quickly. This is where disposition wholesalers come in. They have an extensive network of buyers and marketing channels to quickly sell the properties at a profit.

By working together, acquisition wholesalers and disposition wholesalers can leverage each other's strengths to **maximize profits** and **increase their efficiency**.

Acquisition wholesalers can focus on **finding great deals** while disposition wholesalers can focus on quickly **selling those deals** for a profit. The co-wholesaling partnership allows each party to specialize in their area of expertise while sharing in the profits of the deal. While each wholesaler will earn less on each deal, the end result is that they will each **earn more** because they are able to do more deals together.

This approach allows a new wholesaler to focus on one end of the transaction until they can get to a point where they can do a full wholesale transaction if that's what they want.

3.4 Collaborating with Attorneys and Accountants

As a real estate wholesaler, you will also need to work with attorneys and accountants to ensure that your deals are **legally sound** and **financially viable**. Attorneys can help you to ***review contracts***, ***navigate legal issues***, and protect your interests, while accountants can assist you in ***managing your finances*** and ***preparing tax returns***. To collaborate with attorneys and accountants, it is important to find professionals who are **experienced in real estate law** and finance and who have a track record of success working with wholesalers.

3.5 Developing and Nurturing Relationships with Key Players

Building strong relationships with key players in your wholesaling business is essential to your success. This includes not only real estate agents, attorneys, and accountants, but also potential buyers and sellers. To develop and nurture these relationships, it is important to **communicate regularly**, **provide value**, and **build trust**. This can be done through email, social media, phone calls, or in-person meetings.

Conclusion

In conclusion, building the right team is essential to your success as a real estate wholesaler. By identifying key players, building relationships with real estate agents and brokers, and other wholesalers, collaborating with attorneys and accountants, and developing and nurturing relationships with all key players, you can build a strong and sustainable business that will thrive in the competitive world of wholesale real estate investing.

Chapter 4: Understanding the Market and Finding Deals

To be successful in wholesale real estate investing, you need to have a deep understanding of your market and know how to find great deals in it.

Market - Photo by CHUTTERSNAP

In this chapter, we will discuss how to know your local real estate market, identify motivated sellers, find off-market properties, develop a system for lead generation, and understand deal analysis and estimating property value.

4.1 Knowing Your Local Real Estate Market

One of the most important things you can do as a real estate wholesaler is to know your local market. This means understanding the **current trends**, **property values**, and **demand in your area**. You can do this by researching online, attending local real estate events, and speaking with other professionals in the industry.

Knowing your market will help you to identify potential deals and determine the right price to offer for a property.

4.2 Identifying Motivated Sellers

To find great deals, you need to identify motivated sellers who are willing to sell their property below market value. These can include homeowners facing **foreclosure**, owners of **distressed** or **vacant** properties, and individuals going through a **divorce** or **estate sale**. You can find motivated sellers by marketing to them directly, using online tools and platforms such as Property Radar[1], or working with real estate agents who specialize in distressed properties.

4.3 Finding Off-Market Properties

Off-market properties are properties that are **NOT listed on the MLS** or **other public databases**. These can be great opportunities for real estate wholesalers as they may be available at **below-market prices**.

To find off-market properties, you can use a variety of strategies such as:

1. direct mail campaigns,
2. driving for dollars, and
3. networking with other professionals in the industry.

4.4 Developing a System for Lead Generation

To consistently find great deals, you need to **develop a system** for lead generation. This means setting up a process for ***identifying***, ***tracking***, and ***following up*** on **potential leads**. You can use a variety of tools and software to help automate this process, such as customer relationship management (CRM) software, lead generation software, and email marketing tools such as EngageBay[2].

1. http://jimpellerin.com/propertyradar/

4.5 Understanding Deal Analysis and Estimating Property Value

To be successful in wholesale real estate investing, you need to understand **deal analysis** and how to **estimate property value**. This means knowing how to evaluate a property's condition, determine repair costs, and estimate the potential resale value. You can use online tools, such as DealCheck[3] and Flipster[4], to help estimate property value, or work with experienced real estate professionals to help you evaluate potential deals.

Conclusion

In conclusion, understanding the market and finding great deals is critical to your success as a real estate wholesaler. By knowing your local real estate market, identifying motivated sellers, finding off-market properties, developing a system for lead generation, and understanding deal analysis and estimating property value, you can consistently find great deals and build a thriving wholesaling business.

2. http://jimpellerin.com/engagebay/

3. http://jimpellerin.com/dealcheck/

4. http://jimpellerin.com/flipster/

Chapter 5: Finding Motivated Sellers

Motivated sellers are the **lifeblood** of a successful wholesale real estate investing business. These are individuals who are **motivated to sell** their property quickly, often at a discount, due to a variety of reasons such as financial **distress**, **divorce**, or a **desire to move quickly**.

Motivated Seller - Photo by Yogendra Singh

In this chapter, we will discuss the importance of finding motivated sellers, the different types of motivated sellers, how to leverage marketing strategies to attract them, how to build relationships with them, and navigating the legal and ethical considerations when working with them.

5.1 Understanding the Importance of Finding Motivated Sellers

Finding motivated sellers is **critical to the success of your wholesaling business.** These sellers are often willing to sell their property quickly and at a discount, which can provide you with a greater profit margin on your deals. By having a steady stream of motivated sellers, you can consistently find great deals and build a thriving wholesaling business.

5.2 Identifying Different Types of Motivated Sellers

Motivated sellers can come in many different forms, and it's important to understand the different types so that you can tailor your marketing strategies to reach them effectively. Some common types of motivated sellers include:

- Homeowners facing foreclosure
- Owners of distressed or vacant properties
- Individuals going through a divorce or estate sale
- Property owners with tax liens or other financial burdens
- Owners of properties with code violations or other legal issues

Understanding these different types of motivated sellers can help you to target your marketing efforts and find great deals.

5.3 Leveraging Marketing Strategies to Attract Motivated Sellers

To find motivated sellers, you need to leverage effective marketing strategies. This can include:

- direct mail campaigns,
- online advertising and websites,
- networking with other professionals in the industry, and
- using social media platforms.

It's important to develop a **targeted marketing plan** that reaches the right audience and resonates with their specific needs and motivations.

5.4 Building Relationships with Motivated Sellers

Building relationships with motivated sellers is key to your success as a real estate wholesaler.

This means:

- understanding their needs and motivations,
- listening to their concerns, and
- offering solutions that meet their needs.

By **building trust** and **rapport** with motivated sellers, you can become their go-to resource for their real estate needs and earn their business.

5.5 Navigating Legal and Ethical Considerations When Working with Motivated Sellers

When working with motivated sellers, it's important to navigate the **legal and ethical considerations** involved.

This includes:

1. ensuring that you are complying with all relevant laws and regulations,
2. being transparent and honest in your dealings, and
3. treating motivated sellers with respect and professionalism.

By adhering to these standards, you can build a reputation as a trustworthy and ethical real estate wholesaler.

Conclusion

In conclusion, finding motivated sellers is critical to your success as a real estate wholesaler. By understanding the importance of finding motivated sellers, identifying the different types, leveraging marketing strategies to attract them, building relationships with them, and navigating the legal and ethical considerations involved, you can consistently find great deals and build a thriving wholesaling business.

Chapter 6: Negotiating with Sellers and Buyers

Negotiating is a crucial skill in wholesale real estate investing. In this chapter, we will discuss the essential techniques required to negotiate with sellers and buyers effectively.

Negotiation - Photo by LinkedIn Sales Solutions

6.1 Basic Negotiation Techniques with Sellers

To negotiate with sellers, you need to have a basic understanding of their wants and needs. **Active listening** and **asking the right questions** will help you identify their motivation and pain points. Once you know what they need, you can tailor your offer accordingly. Effective communication, being empathetic, and establishing trust can help you negotiate successfully.

6.2 Building Rapport with Sellers and Finding Win-Win Solutions

Building rapport is essential to establish trust with sellers. Try to connect with them on a personal level, and make them feel comfortable with you. Finding **win-win solutions** means finding solutions that are beneficial to both parties. Understand the seller's situation and present your offer in a way that meets their needs and your own.

6.3 Identifying Common Seller Objections and How to Overcome Them

Sellers may have **objections**, such as not being satisfied with the ***price***, ***time frame***, or other issues. Understanding and addressing these objections effectively can help you close deals. For example, if the seller is not happy with the price, you can justify your offer by providing market data and repair costs.

6.4 Negotiating with Buyers

Negotiating with buyers requires different techniques. You need to be assertive, confident and have a clear understanding of the property's value. Don't be afraid to **reject lowball offers**, and try to negotiate for better terms and conditions.

6.5 Closing Deals with Buyers and Sellers

Once you've negotiated with both parties, you need to **finalize the deal**. Ensure that all parties have agreed on the terms and conditions and that you have a signed contract with both parties. Make sure you follow the legal requirements for wholesaling in your state.

6.6 Understanding the Legal Aspects of Wholesaling

Understanding the legal aspects of wholesaling is crucial to avoid legal issues. You need to be aware of the **state and federal laws** that govern wholesale real estate investing. Ensure that you comply with all legal requirements, such as having a real estate license or using the right contracts.

Conclusion

Negotiation is a critical component of wholesale real estate investing. Developing your negotiation skills can help you close more deals, and create a reputation as a reliable wholesaler. By understanding the seller's and buyer's **needs** and **establishing trust**, you can create win-win situations and close deals successfully.

Chapter 7: Evaluating Properties for Wholesaling

Evaluating properties for wholesaling is a crucial step in the process of wholesale real estate investing. It involves analyzing the property to determine its market value, its potential for profit, and whether it meets your investment goals.

Evaluating - Photo by Karolina Grabowska

This chapter will discuss the different property valuation methods, the financial aspects of wholesaling, and how to conduct due diligence on properties to make informed decisions.

The valuation process is simple and easy to learn. Also, keep in mind, as a wholesaler you will be assigning your contracts to a fix and flipper who will be doing their own valuation so don't spend a lot of time on this step.

7.1 Understanding Property Valuation Methods

As an individual who operates as a wholesaler, it is imperative that you possess the ability to accurately and effectively calculate the **after-repair value (ARV)** of a property. This is a crucial aspect of the wholesaling process, as it allows you to determine the potential profitability of a property and make informed decisions regarding its purchase and resale.

In order to calculate the after-repair value, it is necessary to look at the local real estate market and calculate the average cost per square foot of comparable properties that have recently sold in the area. Then multiply the average cost per square foot by the number of square feet in the subject property. The result is the estimated after-repair value of the property you are evaluating. Check out this free calculator[1] that will assist you in this calculation.

7.2 What is the Maximum Allowable Offer?

When it comes to wholesaling investment, one of the most important factors to consider is the **maximum allowable offer (MAO)**. This is the maximum amount that an investor can offer to purchase a property while still ensuring that they make a profit. Calculating the MAO requires a thorough understanding of the market, the property's condition, and the potential for future profit.

To calculate the MAO, an investor must first determine the after-repair value (ARV) of the property (see previous section). This is the estimated value of the property after it has been repaired and renovated. The ARV can be determined by looking at comparable properties in the area that have recently sold or by consulting with a real estate agent.

1. https://jimpellerin.com/mao-calculator-lp/

Once the ARV has been determined, the wholesaler must then subtract the estimated **repair costs**, **carrying costs**, **assignment fee,** and **profit** from the ARV. This will give them the maximum amount that they can offer for the property which will ensure that there is a profit for the investor. The estimated repair costs should be based on an inspection of the property and should take into account any necessary repairs or renovations.

MAO = ARV - Repair Costs - Carrying Costs - Assignment Fee - Profit

Overall, calculating the MAO requires a careful analysis of the property and the market. Check out this free tool[2] you can use to assist in the MAO calculation.

It is important for wholesalers to take their time and consider all of the relevant factors before making an offer. By doing so, they can ensure that they make a sound offer and maximize the potential profit.

7.3 Other Key Factors that Impact Property Value

When it comes to determining the value of a property, there are several other factors that come into play besides price. Among these factors, the ***location***, ***condition***, and ***size*** of the property are some of the most significant.

In order to make informed decisions about which properties have the potential to generate a high profit margin, it is essential to evaluate these factors carefully and thoroughly. By doing so, wholesalers can identify properties that are likely to sell the fastest, as well as those that may require significant repairs or renovations in order to maximize their profitability.

2. https://jimpellerin.com/mao-calculator-lp/

Location

One of the key considerations when evaluating a property is its **location**. Properties that are situated in **desirable neighborhoods** or areas with **high demand** are generally more valuable than those in less desirable locations. This is because location can impact a wide range of factors, including ***access to amenities***, ***transportation options***, and the ***overall quality of life*** in the area. As such, wholesalers should carefully consider the location of a property before making any decisions.

Property Condition

Another important factor to consider when evaluating a property is its **condition**. Properties that are in **good condition** and require **minimal repairs** or renovations are generally more valuable than those that are in poor condition. This is because properties that are in good condition are more likely to attract buyers, and are less likely to require costly repairs or maintenance. As such, wholesalers should carefully inspect a property's condition before making any offer.

Property Size

Finally, the **size** of a property is also an important consideration when evaluating its value. Properties that are larger in size are generally **more valuable** than those that are smaller, as they offer more space and potential for higher resale value. However, wholesalers should also consider the cost of repairing a larger property, as well as the potential for longer sales times as there is less of a demand for larger homes.

Other Considerations

In addition to these factors, it is also important to be aware of any hidden problems that may impact a property's value and profitability. These can include issues such as **structural damage**, **pest infestations**, or **zoning restrictions** that may impact the property's profit potential.

By carefully evaluating these factors and conducting thorough **due diligence**, wholesalers can identify properties that have the potential to generate a high profit margin and avoid those that may pose a risk to any investor.

7.4 Conducting Due Diligence on Properties

It is essential to conduct due diligence to ensure that the property is worth the investment. Due diligence refers to the process of investigating and verifying the property's ***legal***, ***financial***, and ***physical*** aspects to identify any potential risks or issues that may affect the purchase decision. The activities required to do due diligence before buying a house involve a comprehensive and meticulous examination of these factors.

Legal

Firstly, it is crucial to review the property's **legal documents**, including the ***title deed***, ***survey report***, and ***zoning regulations***. This step helps to confirm the property's ownership, boundaries, and any restrictions or limitations on its use.

Financial

Secondly, it is necessary to assess the property's **financial aspects**, such as its ***market value***, ***taxes***, and any ***outstanding debts*** or ***liens***. This step helps to determine the property's affordability and potential return on investment.

Physical

Thirdly, it is essential to inspect the property's **physical condition**, including its ***structural integrity***, ***electrical*** and ***plumbing*** systems, and any potential ***hazards*** or ***defects***. This step helps to identify any necessary repairs or renovations and estimate their costs.

Neighborhood

Additionally, it is advisable to conduct a **neighborhood analysis** to evaluate the area's ***safety***, ***accessibility***, and ***amenities***. This step helps to determine the property's suitability for the end-buyer's lifestyle and preferences.

Overall, conducting due diligence before buying a house is a critical process that requires careful attention to detail and thorough investigation. By completing these activities, wholesalers and buyers can make informed decisions and avoid potential risks or issues that may arise after the purchase.

7.5 Knowing When to Walk Away from a Deal

Not all deals are good deals, and wholesalers need to know when to walk away from a deal.

As a wholesaler, it is imperative to have a keen eye for identifying profitable deals. However, not all deals that come your way are worth pursuing, and it is crucial to know when to walk away from a deal.

In this section, we will discuss the red flags that indicate a deal may not be worth pursuing, including properties that have **too many problems**, properties that are **overpriced**, and properties that are in **undesirable locations**.

We will also explain how to calculate the **potential profit** margin to determine whether a deal is worth pursuing.

Too Many Problems

One of the most significant red flags is a property that has **too many problems**. These problems could range from ***structural issues*** to ***legal complications***, and they can significantly impact the profitability of the deal. It is essential to conduct a thorough inspection of the property and assess the extent of the problems before making a decision.

Overpriced

Another red flag to watch out for is properties that are **overpriced**. While it is natural for sellers to want to get the best price for their property, it is crucial to ensure that the price is **reasonable and within market value**. Overpriced properties can be challenging to assign and sell, and you may end up stuck with the property in the long run.

Undesirable Locations

Properties that are in **undesirable locations** are also a red flag. These locations could be in ***high-crime areas***, ***flood-prone areas***, or areas with ***poor infrastructure***. Such properties may be challenging to sell, and the buyer may end up holding onto them for an extended period, which can be costly and effects the overall profit.

Potential Profit

To determine whether a deal is worth pursuing, it is essential to calculate the **potential profit** margin. This involves assessing the ***purchase price***, ***repair costs***, and the ***expected selling price***. If the potential profit margin is low, it may not be worth pursuing the deal.

In conclusion, as a wholesaler, it is crucial to be vigilant and identify the red flags that indicate a deal may not be worth pursuing. By doing so, you can save yourself time, effort, and money and focus on deals that have the potential to yield significant profits.

Conclusion

Evaluating properties for wholesaling is a critical step in the wholesaling process. This chapter has discussed the different property valuation methods, the financial aspects of wholesaling, how to conduct due diligence on properties, and how to make informed decisions about which properties to invest in.

Chapter 8: Marketing Your Wholesale Properties

Marketing your wholesale properties is an essential part of your wholesaling business. Without proactive and effective marketing, you may **struggle to find buyers** for your properties.

Marketing - Photo by PhotoMIX-Company

In this chapter, you will learn about the different strategies and techniques for marketing your wholesale properties.

8.1 Developing a Marketing Strategy for Your Properties

The first step in marketing your wholesale properties is to develop a **marketing strategy**. This involves ***identifying your target market***, ***determining the best channels*** to reach them, and ***creating a plan*** to promote your properties. Your marketing strategy should include a **mix of online and offline marketing techniques**, such as property listings, social media promotion, email marketing, direct mail, and more.

8.2 Creating Effective Property Listings and Descriptions

Your property listings and descriptions are critical to attracting potential buyers. Your listings should be descriptive and **showcase the unique features** of each property. Additionally, you should include high-quality photos and videos to give buyers a better idea of what the property looks like. Also, you should have the financials already figured out and include them in your presentations. This includes ARV, asking price, estimated renovation costs, potential profit for the buyer, and your assignment fee.

8.3 Developing Relationships with Potential Buyers

The best marketing plan is to not need one. **Building relationships with potential buyers** in advance is an essential part of marketing your wholesale properties. You can attend local real estate events and networking groups to meet potential buyers or reach out to buyers directly through email or phone. Be sure to keep your buyer database up to date and follow up with leads regularly. Facebook groups are a goldmine of potential buyers.

8.4 Using Social Media to Promote Your Properties

Social media is a powerful tool for marketing your wholesale properties. You can use platforms like ***Facebook***, ***Twitter***, and ***Instagram*** to showcase your properties and connect with potential buyers. Consider running targeted ads to reach a wider audience and using **social media groups** to network with other real estate professionals.

8.5 Leveraging Technology to Streamline Your Marketing Efforts

Technology can help you streamline your marketing efforts and save time. For example, you can use marketing automation tools[1] to schedule social media posts, send out email newsletters, and perform other marketing activities. Use a tool like DealCheck[2] to create professional-looking presentations. Additionally, you can use virtual tours and video walkthroughs to showcase your properties to potential buyers.

Conclusion

Marketing your wholesale properties effectively is essential for the success of your wholesaling business. By developing a **comprehensive marketing strategy** and leveraging the latest marketing techniques and tools, you can reach a wider audience and find buyers for your properties quickly and easily.

1. http://jimpellerin.com/engagebay/
2. http://jimpellerin.com/dealcheck/

Chapter 9: Building Your Wholesaling Real Estate Brand

Building your wholesaling real estate brand is a crucial step in establishing your business and attracting potential buyers and sellers. In this chapter, we will explore the key steps to creating and developing a strong brand identity that stands out in a crowded market.

Branding - Photo by Eva Bronzini

9.1 Establishing Your Brand Identity

The first step to building a successful brand is to establish your brand identity. This includes defining your company's values, mission statement, and overall image. Your brand identity should reflect your personality, values, and what **sets you apart from other wholesalers**. A strong brand identity can help create trust and credibility with your clients, which can lead to increased sales and referrals.

9.2 Developing Your Brand Messaging

Your brand messaging is the way you communicate your brand identity to the world. It should be **clear**, **concise**, and **consistent** across all your marketing materials. Your messaging should convey your unique selling proposition (USP) and the benefits of working with your company. Your messaging should also address the pain points of your target audiences and how your services can solve their problems.

9.3 Creating a Website and Other Marketing Collateral

Creating a professional website[1] and marketing materials is essential to building your brand. Your website should reflect your **brand identity** and include your USP and messaging. It should be easy to navigate, visually appealing, and optimized for search engines. The best website builder for wholesaling and motivated sellers that I have found is Carrot.

Other marketing materials, such as business cards, brochures, and flyers, should also reflect your brand identity and messaging.

9.4 Building a Social Media Presence

Social media is a powerful tool for building your brand and engaging with potential clients. You should identify which platforms your target audience is most active on and create a **social media strategy** that aligns with your brand identity and messaging. For buyers, I would focus on ***Linkedin***, ***Facebook*** and ***Facebook Groups*** that focus on real estate investing or wholesaling in your area. Consistency is key, and you should post regularly and engage with your followers to build a strong online presence.

1. http://jimpellerin.com/carrot/

9.5 Differentiating Yourself from Competitors

Differentiating yourself from your competitors is essential to building a strong brand. You should identify what makes you **unique** and emphasize those qualities in your messaging and marketing materials. Maybe you specialize in a certain geographical area or in foreclosures. This could be your USP, your approach to customer service, or your experience in the industry.

9.6 Leveraging Testimonials and Referrals to Build Your Reputation

Testimonials and referrals are powerful tools for building your reputation and establishing credibility with potential clients. You should encourage satisfied clients to leave **reviews and testimonials** on your website and social media platforms. You should also **ask for referrals** from your satisfied clients and offer incentives for them to refer their friends and family.

Conclusion

Building a strong brand identity is essential to the success of your wholesaling business. By establishing your brand identity, developing your brand messaging, and identifying your USP, you can create a powerful brand that stands out in a crowded market. By creating a professional website and marketing materials, building a social media presence, differentiating yourself from your competitors, and leveraging testimonials and referrals, you can build a strong reputation and attract potential clients.

Chapter 10: Developing a Mindset for Success

Developing a mindset for success is one of the most critical aspects of becoming a successful real estate wholesaler. The right mindset can help you **overcome obstacles, take calculated risks**, and **stay motivated** during challenging times.

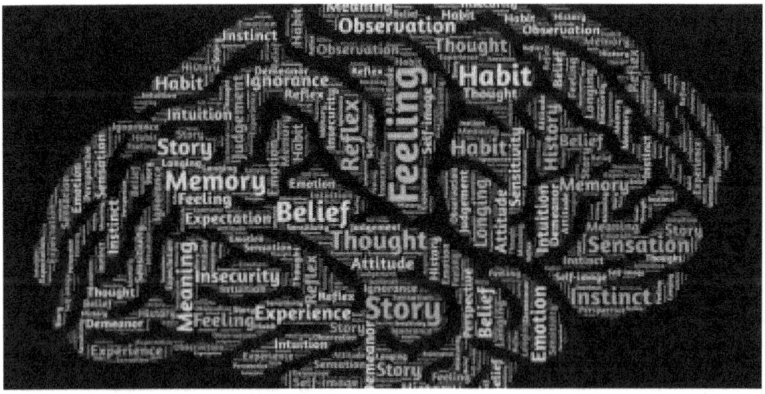

Mindset - Photo by johnhain

In this chapter, we will explore the key elements of developing a successful mindset.

10.1 Adopting a Growth Mindset

Adopting a growth mindset means embracing the idea that you can always improve and grow, no matter your current level of expertise. Successful real estate wholesalers understand that there is **always something to learn**, and they approach every situation as an opportunity to gain knowledge and experience. A growth mindset also means that you are **willing to take risks**, even if it means making mistakes along the way.

10.2 Overcoming Fear and Doubt

Fear and doubt are common barriers to success in any industry, and wholesale real estate investing is no exception. To be successful, you must learn how to overcome these emotions and move forward despite them. One effective way to overcome fear and doubt is to **focus on your goals** and why you want to achieve them. Keep in mind that every successful wholesaler has faced fear and doubt at some point and has learned how to overcome them. You will experience lots of rejection from not-so-motivated sellers but you must **persevere** and keep talking to sellers in hopes of finding motivated sellers that are looking for your assistance.

10.3 Staying Motivated During Challenging Times

Wholesale real estate investing can be a challenging and unpredictable business, and it's essential to stay motivated during difficult times. One way to do this is to **focus on your "why."** Why did you get into wholesale real estate investing in the first place? What motivates you to keep going, even when things get tough? By staying connected to your motivation, you can push through difficult times and stay focused on your goals.

10.4 Celebrating Small Wins

Celebrating small wins is an important part of developing a successful mindset. Every successful real estate wholesaler knows that achieving significant goals takes time and effort, and it's important to acknowledge and **celebrate progress** along the way. Celebrating small wins can help you stay motivated and build momentum toward your larger goals. Some examples are contacting your 100th seller or getting your 100th no.

10.5 Setting and Achieving Realistic Goals:

Setting and achieving realistic goals is critical for success in wholesale real estate investing. Your goals should be specific, measurable, and achievable within a set timeframe. It's essential to break larger goals down into **smaller, more manageable steps**, and to regularly assess your progress towards those goals. By setting and achieving realistic goals, you can build confidence, stay motivated, and ultimately achieve the success you desire.

Conclusion

Developing a successful mindset is a critical component of becoming a successful real estate wholesaler. By adopting a growth mindset, overcoming fear and doubt, staying motivated during challenging times, celebrating small wins, and setting and achieving realistic goals, you can develop the mindset necessary for success. Remember that success in wholesale real estate investing takes time, effort, and dedication, but with the right mindset, anything is possible.

Chapter 11: Managing Your Wholesaling Deals

Managing your wholesaling deals is an essential part of a successful wholesale real estate investing business. It is essential to have a **well-organized and efficient system** for managing your deals to ensure that you can handle all the necessary tasks and keep everything running smoothly.

Manage - Photo by geralt

11.1 Developing a System for Managing Your Deals

Developing a **system** for managing your deals is the first step in successfully managing your wholesaling deals. Your system should include all the necessary steps and tasks required for the wholesaling process, from identifying potential properties to closing the deal.

To develop an **effective system**, start by breaking down the wholesaling process into its different stages and creating a checklist for each stage.

Each stage should include all the necessary **tasks**, **timelines**, and **deadlines** required to complete the stage successfully.

Your system should also include a way to **track your progress** and monitor your deals' status.

11.2 Staying Organized and Efficient with Deal Management

To **manage** your wholesaling deals efficiently, it is essential to stay organized and focused. This can be achieved by developing a routine and sticking to it. Create a **daily schedule** that includes time for ***lead generation***, ***follow-up calls***, ***property inspections***, and ***deal management*** tasks.

Make sure to prioritize your tasks based on their importance and urgency. Focus on completing the most critical tasks first and **delegate** less important tasks to other team members or contractors.

To stay organized, consider using a project management tool, such as Team Gantt[1] or ClickUp[2] to manage your tasks and track progress. These tools can help you stay on top of all your deals and ensure that nothing falls through the cracks.

11.3 Communicating Effectively with Buyers and Sellers

Effective communication is essential for successful deal management. It is crucial to **keep buyers and sellers informed** throughout the entire process and to be transparent and honest about any issues or challenges that arise.

Make sure to establish clear **communication channels** and keep all parties involved in the deal updated on its progress. Use email, phone

1. http://jimpellerin.com/teamgantt/

2. http://jimpellerin.com/clickup/

calls, and text messages to keep in touch with buyers and sellers and to answer any questions they may have.

When communicating with buyers and sellers, be **professional** and **respectful** at all times. Remember that you are representing your business, and your communication skills will directly impact your reputation.

11.4 Handling Challenges and Obstacles During Deals

Wholesale real estate investing deals can be complicated and challenging, and it is essential to be prepared to handle any **challenges** or **obstacles** that may arise. To manage these challenges effectively, stay calm and level-headed, and don't let your emotions get the best of you.

Be **proactive** in addressing issues and challenges and develop a plan to overcome them. Reach out to your network of contacts, such as ***attorneys***, ***real estate agents***, and ***contractors***, for help and advice if necessary.

When facing challenges, stay focused on **finding solutions** rather than dwelling on the problem. Use your problem-solving skills to find creative solutions and keep your deals on track.

11.5 Celebrating Successes and Learning from Mistakes in Your Wholesaling Deals

Finally, it is essential to **celebrate your successes** and **learn from your mistakes** in your wholesaling deals. Take the time to acknowledge your achievements and recognize the hard work that went into closing a successful deal.

At the same time, use your mistakes and failures as opportunities to learn and grow. Analyze what went wrong and identify areas where you can improve your process or strategy in the future.

Conclusion

Managing your wholesaling deals effectively requires a combination of organization, communication, and problem-solving skills. By developing a system for managing your deals, staying organized and efficient, communicating effectively with buyers and sellers, and handling challenges and obstacles.

Chapter 12: Scaling Your Business

Scaling your wholesaling business involves growing it by increasing its ***size***, ***revenue***, and ***profitability***. It can also mean expanding into ***new markets*** and diversifying your business offerings. However, scaling a business requires **planning**, **resources**, and a **strategic approach**. Scaling will cost you money for resources and people.

Scaling Business - Photo by marcelrmlsp

In this chapter, we will explore the steps you can take to scale your wholesaling business successfully.

12.1 Knowing When to Scale Your Business

Scaling your wholesaling business should not be taken lightly as it requires ***resources***, ***capital***, and ***time***. It's crucial to determine whether you are ready to scale your business before you take the plunge. Some signs that indicate you're ready to scale include:

- **Consistent profits:** Your business should be generating consistent profits that can support growth.

- **High demand:** If there is a high demand for your services, scaling your business can help you meet this demand.
- **Capacity:** Your business should have the capacity to handle growth without compromising on quality or customer service. Outsource or hire help.
- **Repeatable processes:** Scaling your business requires repeatable processes that can be scaled without reducing quality or efficiency when assigned to someone else.
- **Market opportunity:** If you have identified an untapped market, scaling your business can help you reach that market and capitalize on the opportunity.

12.2 Developing a Plan for Growth

Once you've decided to scale your business, it's essential to develop a growth plan that outlines your goals, strategies, and tactics. Your growth plan should include the following elements:

- **Identify your target market:** Determine your target market and research their needs and preferences. Foreclosures, disgruntled landlords, etc.
- **Develop a marketing plan:** Create a marketing plan that outlines how you will reach your target market and promote your services.
- **Determine your fee structure:** Determine your fee structure based on your market research and competition.
- **Build a team:** Build a team of professionals who can support your business's growth, including salespeople, marketers, and operations staff.
- **Plan your finances:** Plan your finances carefully, including your budget, revenue projections, and cash flow.
- **Develop operational systems:** Develop operational systems

that can support growth, including lead generation, acquisitions, and dispositions.

12.3 Identifying Potential Risks and Challenges

Scaling your business comes with inherent risks and challenges. Some of the potential risks and challenges you may face include:

- **Cash flow problems:** Scaling your business requires capital, and you may experience cash flow problems during the growth phase.
- **Supply chain issues:** As your business grows, you may face supply chain issues, including finding enough motivated sellers and properties.
- **Staffing problems:** Scaling your business requires a team of professionals, and you may face staffing problems, including finding the right talent and retaining them.
- **Operational inefficiencies:** As your business grows, you may experience operational inefficiencies, including a lack of standardization, communication problems, and process bottlenecks.
- **Increased competition:** As your business expands, you may face increased competition from new entrants in the market.

Identifying these risks and challenges in advance can help you develop strategies to mitigate them.

12.4 Building a Team to Support Your Growth

Scaling your business requires a team of professionals who can support your growth. You may need to **hire new employees**, **outsource work**, or **partner with other wholesalers**. Some of the key professionals you may need include:

- **Marketers:** Marketers can help you develop and implement marketing strategies that can help you reach your target market.
- **Salespeople:** Salespeople can help you reach new markets and increase your revenue.
- **Operations staff:** Operations staff can help you manage your properties, contracts, and back-end systems.
- **Advisors:** Advisors can provide guidance and support as you scale your business, including legal, financial, and strategic advice.

Building a strong team can help you navigate the challenges of growth.

12.5 Leveraging Technology and Automation to Scale

Technology and automation can play a crucial role in scaling your business. By automating repetitive tasks and leveraging technology, you can increase efficiency, reduce costs, and improve customer service. Some of the ways you can leverage technology and automation include:

Using customer relationship management [1](CRM) software: CRM software can help you manage customer interactions and improve customer service.

Implementing lead generation software[2]: Lead generation software can help you locate motivated sellers and manage your outreach to these potential customers.

Conclusion

In conclusion, scaling your business requires careful planning, resources, and a strategic approach. By knowing when to scale,

1. http://jimpellerin.com/engagebay/

2. http://jimpellerin.com/propertyradar/

developing a growth plan, identifying potential risks and challenges, building a strong team, and leveraging technology and automation, you can successfully scale your wholesaling business and achieve your growth goals.

Chapter 13: Networking and Building Relationships

Wholesale real estate investing is a people business, and building a strong network of contacts is essential to success. Networking and **building relationships** can help wholesalers to find ***motivated sellers***, connect with ***potential buyers***, and build partnerships with other ***professionals*** in the industry.

Networking - Photo by Product School

In this chapter, we will explore some strategies for building a strong network of contacts and staying connected with them.

13.1 Building a Strong Network of Contacts

Building a strong network of contacts is crucial for success in wholesale real estate investing. The more people you know, the more opportunities you will have to find deals, connect with buyers and sellers, and build partnerships with other professionals in the industry.

One way to build a strong network of contacts is to **attend local real estate events** and meetings. This includes ***real estate investor associations***, ***industry conferences***, and other ***networking events***.

Attending these events allows you to meet other **wholesalers**, **investors**, and **professionals** in the industry. It's a great way to make connections and learn about the latest trends and strategies in real estate.

Another way to build your network is to **join real estate investment groups**. These groups typically consist of like-minded individuals who are interested in investing in real estate. Joining an investment group can help you to find potential buyers and partners for your deals. It's also a great way to learn from other investors and wholesalers in the industry.

13.2 Attending Real Estate Industry Events

Attending real estate industry events is an excellent way to build your network of contacts. Industry events provide an opportunity to meet other wholesalers, investors, and professionals in the industry. These events often feature keynote speakers, educational sessions, and networking opportunities.

Attending these events can also help you to stay current on **industry trends** and **meet other professionals** who can help you to grow your business. It's also a great way to build relationships with potential buyers and other wholesalers.

13.3 Joining Real Estate Investment Groups

Joining a real estate investment group is another way to build your network of contacts. These groups typically consist of **investors and**

wholesalers who are interested in investing in real estate. Joining a group can help you to find potential buyers and partners for your deals.

It's also an excellent way to **learn** from other investors and wholesalers in the industry. Many investment groups offer ***educational sessions***, ***mentorship programs***, and ***networking events***. By joining a group, you can learn from experienced professionals and get support as you grow your business.

13.4 Utilizing Online Networking Platforms:

In addition to attending real estate events and joining investment groups, you can also build your network by utilizing **online** networking platforms. Social media platforms like ***LinkedIn***, ***Facebook***, and ***Twitter*** can be a great way to connect with other professionals in the industry.

By joining online real estate groups and forums, you can connect with other wholesalers and investors who **share your interests**. You can also use these platforms to promote your business and build relationships with potential buyers.

13.5 Developing a System for Following Up and Staying Connected

Building a strong network is not just about making connections. It's also about **maintaining those connections** and staying top of mind with your contacts. To do this, you need to develop a system[1] for following up and staying connected.

One way to stay connected with your contacts is to **send regular emails** or **newsletters**. This can help you keep your contacts informed about your business and any new deals you have available. You can also use this opportunity to ask for referrals or recommendations.

1. http://jimpellerin.com/engagebay/

Another way to stay connected is to **schedule regular phone or in-person meetings** with your contacts. This allows you to catch up and discuss any potential deals or partnerships.

Conclusion

Building a strong network of contacts is essential for success in wholesale real estate investing. By attending events, joining investment groups, utilizing online networking platforms, and developing a system for following up, you can build good relationships.

Chapter 14: Expanding Your Wholesaling Reach

Expanding your wholesaling reach can be achieved through **virtual wholesaling** or by targeting **markets outside of your local area.**

Expanding - Photo by GeoJango Maps

The chapter provides an overview of the benefits of expanding your reach, the challenges you may face, and strategies for building relationships with out-of-state investors.

14.1 Understanding the Benefits of Virtual Wholesaling

Virtual wholesaling involves **conducting wholesale deals remotely**, without ever visiting the property or meeting the seller in person. This approach can allow you to expand your reach and do business in different markets **without physically being there**. It can also save you time and money by eliminating the need to travel, reducing expenses related to marketing materials, and making it easier to scale your business. However, virtual wholesaling requires you to have strong communication skills and technical **proficiency** to conduct deals remotely.

14.2 Identifying Markets Outside of Your Local Area

Identifying new markets to target is essential for expanding your wholesaling reach. You can research markets outside of your local area by looking for cities or regions with favorable real estate market conditions, such as **low inventory**, **high demand**, and a **growing population**. Additionally, you may consider looking for markets with emerging industries or job opportunities, as this can increase demand for housing and drive up property values.

14.3 Developing a Strategy for Expanding Your Reach

To successfully expand your reach, you need to have a clear strategy in place. This includes identifying your **target markets**, researching real estate **market conditions**, developing a **marketing pla**n to reach out to potential sellers and buyers, and creating a system for managing deals remotely. It's important to consider the potential challenges of working in a new market, such as unfamiliar regulations, different buying preferences, and increased competition.

14.4 Building Relationships with Out-of-State Investors

To effectively expand your reach, you need to build relationships with investors and wholesalers in your new target markets. You can do this by attending real estate investment events and joining industry groups, such as real estate associations or investor networks. Additionally, you can utilize **online networking platforms**, such as ***LinkedIn*** and ***BiggerPockets***, to connect with potential partners and investors. Building strong relationships can help you gain access to off-market deals, learn about market trends and conditions, and expand your referral network.

14.5 Navigating Legal and Tax Implications of Out-of-State Wholesaling

Expanding your reach to new markets requires you to **understand the legal and tax implications** of wholesaling properties outside of your state. You need to comply with state and federal regulations, such as ***licensing requirements***, ***contract laws***, and ***disclosure requirements***. Additionally, you need to be aware of any differences in state tax laws and consult with a tax professional to ensure compliance.

Conclusion

Expanding your wholesaling reach can be an effective way to grow your business, gain access to new markets, and build relationships with investors and wholesalers. To successfully expand your reach, you need to have a clear strategy in place, develop strong relationships with industry professionals, and stay up-to-date on legal and tax requirements. With the right approach, virtual wholesaling and targeting new markets can help you take your wholesaling business to the next level.

Chapter 15: Leveraging Technology to Streamline Your Business

Technology has revolutionized the real estate industry, and wholesalers can take advantage of it to streamline their business operations.

Technology - Photo by Ales Nesetril

In this chapter, we will explore the different ways wholesalers can leverage technology to improve their workflow and stay ahead of the competition.

15.1 Identifying Technology Tools to Improve Your Workflow

The first step to leveraging technology for your wholesaling business is to identify the tools that can help you streamline your workflow. Some of the technology tools that wholesalers can use include:

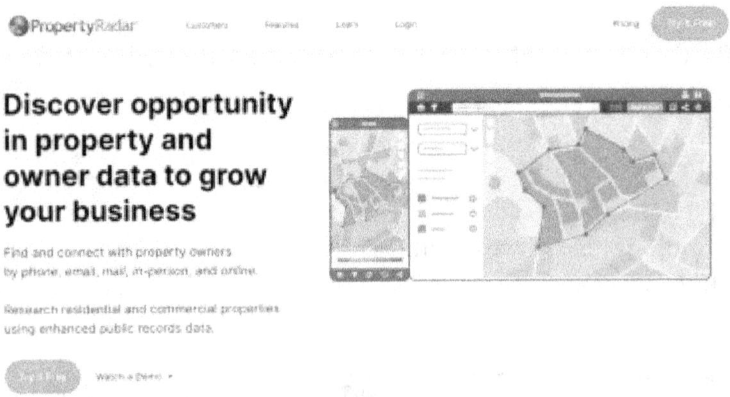

[1]

PropertyRadar

- **Lead Gen Software:** Real estate lead generation software has become an essential tool for real estate professionals looking to find and acquire leads quickly and efficiently. Two examples of such software are Propstream and PropertyRadar. Propstream[2] is a comprehensive real estate platform that provides access to nationwide property data, including ownership information, property characteristics, and transaction history. It also features a robust lead generation tool that allows users to create targeted lists of motivated sellers based on specific criteria such as location, property type, and more. PropertyRadar[3], on the other hand, is a marketing automation platform designed to help real estate professionals find new leads, market to them effectively, and close more deals. It provides detailed property data, and owner information, and even tracks leads' behavioral patterns to help wholesalers tailor their marketing campaigns.

1. http://jimpellerin.com/propertyradar/
2. http://jimpellerin.com/propstream/
3. http://jimpellerin.com/propertyradar/

- **CRM systems:** A Customer Relationship Management (CRM) system is a software solution that allows you to manage all your customer data and interactions in one place. This tool can help wholesalers track leads, manage contacts, and automate follow-up tasks. Some popular CRM systems you can use for real estate include EngageBay[4], Simpli[5], and REI Blackbook[6].
- **Project management software:** This tool can help wholesalers manage their projects and tasks more efficiently. Project management software allows wholesalers to assign tasks, track progress, and collaborate with team members. Some popular project management software options include Team Gantt[7] and ClickUp[8].
- **Real Estate Analysis Software:** Real estate analysis software has become an essential tool for real estate wholesalers looking to analyze potential deals quickly and accurately. Two examples of such software are DealCheck and Flipster.

DealCheck[9] is a powerful real estate analysis tool that allows investors to evaluate the financial viability of a potential deal by inputting relevant data such as property value, rental income, and expenses. It can also factor in various metrics like cash-on-cash return, cap rate, and internal rate of return, making it easier for investors to make informed decisions about their investments.

---

4. http://jimpellerin.com/engagebay/
5. https://jimpellerin.com/simpli
6. http://jimpellerin.com/reiblackbook/
7. http://jimpellerin.com/teamgantt/
8. http://jimpellerin.com/clickup/
9. http://jimpellerin.com/dealcheck/

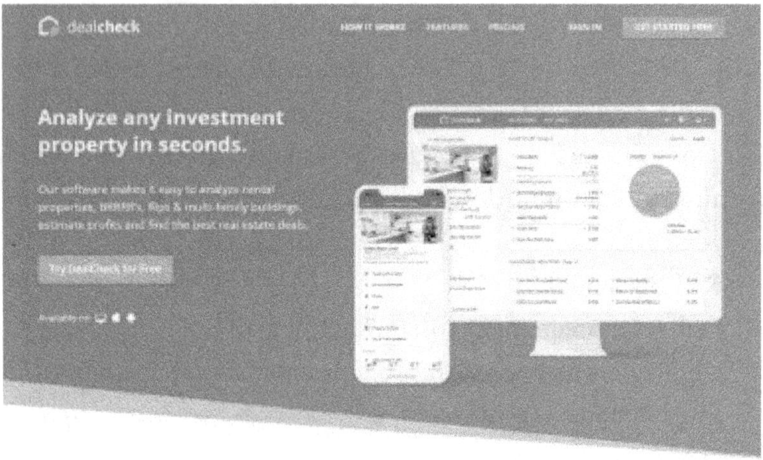

[10]

Flipster[11], on the other hand, is a software platform designed specifically for real estate flippers. It includes tools for analyzing potential deals, estimating rehab costs, and tracking expenses throughout the renovation process. It also provides customizable project timelines and budgets, making it easier for investors to stay on track and on budget.

[12]

10. http://jimpellerin.com/dealcheck/

11. http://jimpellerin.com/flipster/

12. http://jimpellerin.com/flipster/

15.2 Using Customer Relationship Management (CRM) Systems

A CRM system[13] can be a game-changer for wholesalers looking to streamline their business operations. With a CRM system, wholesalers can manage all their customer data in one place, making it easier to track leads, manage contacts, and automate follow-up tasks.

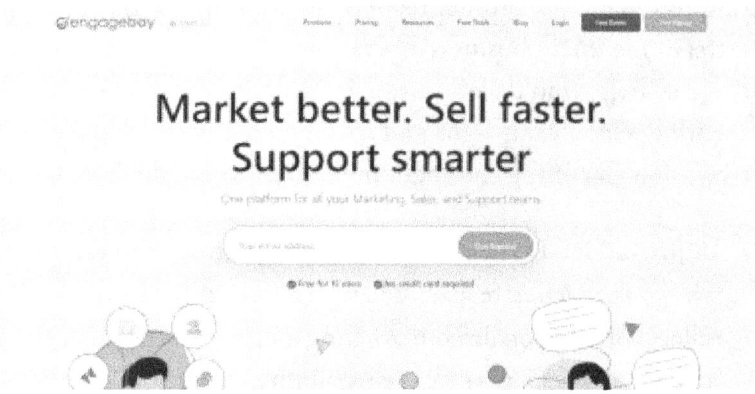

[14]

Some of the benefits of using a CRM system for wholesaling include:

- **Improved lead tracking:** A CRM system can help wholesalers track leads from multiple sources, such as online ads, referrals, and direct mail campaigns. This tool can help wholesalers identify which lead sources are most effective, allowing them to focus their marketing efforts where it matters most.
- **Enhanced communication:** A CRM system can help wholesalers keep track of all their communication with buyers and sellers. This tool can help wholesalers stay organized and ensure that no leads fall through the cracks.
- **Automated follow-up:** A CRM system can automate follow-

13. http://jimpellerin.com/engagebay/

14. http://jimpellerin.com/engagebay/

up tasks such as sending emails and reminders, allowing wholesalers to focus on other aspects of their business. Automated follow-up can help wholesalers save time and increase their chances of closing deals.

15.3 Implementing Marketing Automation

Marketing automation is another technology tool that wholesalers can use to streamline their business operations. Marketing automation software[15] can help wholesalers automate repetitive marketing tasks, such as sending email campaigns and social media posts. Some of the benefits of using marketing automation for wholesaling include:

- **Improved lead generation:** Marketing automation can help wholesalers generate leads by targeting potential buyers and sellers with personalized marketing messages. This tool can help wholesalers increase their visibility and attract new leads.
- **Increased efficiency:** Marketing automation can help wholesalers save time by automating repetitive marketing tasks. This tool can free up time for wholesalers to focus on other aspects of their business, such as deal-making and relationship-building.
- **Enhanced personalization:** Marketing automation can help wholesalers personalize their marketing messages based on customer data. This tool can help wholesalers create more effective marketing campaigns that resonate with their target audience.

15. http://jimpellerin.com/engagebay/

15.4 Leveraging Data Analytics for Decision-Making

Data analytics is the process of using data to inform decision-making and improve performance. In the context of wholesaling, data analytics can be used to **analyze market trends**, **track sales performance**, and **identify areas for improvement**. By leveraging data analytics, wholesalers can make informed decisions that will help them improve their business and stay ahead of the competition.

There are several types of data analytics that wholesalers can use, including **descriptive**, **predictive**, and **prescriptive** analytics.

1. **Descriptive analytics** involves analyzing historical data to understand what has happened in the ***past***.
2. **Predictive analytics** uses statistical algorithms and machine learning to make predictions about ***future*** events based on past data.
3. **Prescriptive analytics** takes things a step further by recommending specific actions to ***improve*** outcomes.

To get started with data analytics, wholesalers should begin by identifying the key performance indicators (KPIs) that are most important to their business. This might include metrics like the number of **leads generated**, **conversion rates**, or **average deal size**. Once these KPIs have been identified, wholesalers can begin collecting and analyzing data to track their performance over time.

There are many tools available to help wholesalers with data analytics, including CRM software[16], marketing automation platforms, and data visualization tools[17]. These tools can help wholesalers collect, analyze, and visualize data in a way that is easy to understand and use.

---

16. http://jimpellerin.com/engagebay/

17. http://jimpellerin.com/propertyradar/

15.5 Staying Up-to-Date with Emerging Technologies

Technology is constantly evolving, and it is important for wholesalers to stay up-to-date with the latest developments in order to remain competitive. This might include adopting new tools and software, exploring emerging technologies like **artificial intelligence** and blockchain, or keeping up with industry trends and best practices.

To stay up-to-date with emerging technologies, wholesalers can **attend industry conferences** and events, **read industry publications** and blogs, and **network with other professionals** in the field. They can also take advantage of online resources like webinars, podcasts, and online courses to learn about new technologies and best practices.

In addition to staying up-to-date with emerging technologies, wholesalers should also be open to **experimentation** and **innovation**. By testing new ideas and approaches, wholesalers can discover new ways to improve their business and stay ahead of the competition.

Conclusion

Wholesaling can be a lucrative and rewarding business, but it requires a combination of hard work, determination, and strategic thinking to succeed. By following the strategies outlined in this guide, wholesalers can develop the skills, knowledge, and mindset they need to succeed in the competitive world of wholesale real estate investing. Whether you are just starting out or are looking to take your business to the next level, this guide provides a comprehensive roadmap for success in wholesaling.

Chapter 16: Avoiding Common Wholesaling Mistakes

Avoiding mistakes is critical in any business, and wholesaling is no exception. In this chapter, we will explore common wholesaling mistakes and how to avoid them. By learning from the mistakes of others, you can save time and money, and increase your chances of success.

Upside Down House - Photo by ocd studio

16.1 Identifying Common Wholesaling Mistakes

The following are some common mistakes that wholesalers make:

- Not researching the market thoroughly before making a purchase
- Overestimating the after-repair value (ARV) of a property
- Underestimating the repair costs of a property
- Failing to perform due diligence on a property
- Not having a solid contract in place before looking for buyers

- Not building relationships with buyers and sellers
- Not having a clear exit strategy in place before making an offer
- Failing to follow up with buyers and sellers
- Not being prepared for unexpected expenses or delays

By identifying these common mistakes, you can take proactive measures to avoid them.

16.2 Learning from Your Mistakes and Challenges

Mistakes and challenges are inevitable in any business, including wholesaling. The key is to learn from them and use the lessons learned to improve your business. One way to do this is to **keep a log** of your mistakes and challenges and what you learned from them. Regularly reviewing this log can help you identify patterns and develop strategies to prevent similar mistakes in the future.

16.3 Building Resilience and Persistence

Wholesaling can be a challenging business, and it is essential to build **resilience** and **persistence** to overcome **obstacles** and **setbacks**. One way to do this is to set **realistic goals** and celebrate small successes along the way. This can help you stay motivated and focused on your long-term goals. Additionally, it is crucial to have a support system in place, such as a ***mentor*** or a network of other investors who can offer advice and encouragement.

16.4 Implementing Processes to Avoid Repeating Mistakes

Once you have identified common mistakes and learned from your own mistakes and challenges, it is crucial to **implement processes** to avoid repeating them. This can include creating checklists and standard operating procedures (SOPs) for tasks such as **property inspections** and due diligence. It can also involve establishing clear communication and documentation procedures to ensure that all parties are on the same page throughout the transaction.

16.5 Knowing When to Seek Help and Guidance

Finally, it is essential to know when to seek help and guidance. This can include reaching out to **other investors** for advice, hiring a **mentor** or **coach**, or consulting with **legal and financial professionals**. By seeking help and guidance when needed, you can avoid costly mistakes and improve your chances of success.

Conclusion

Avoiding common wholesaling mistakes is critical to the success of your business. By identifying these mistakes, learning from your own mistakes and challenges, building resilience and persistence, implementing processes to avoid repeating mistakes, and seeking help and guidance when needed, you can increase your chances of success in the wholesaling business.

Chapter 17: Wholesale Real Estate Investing and the Future of the Industry

As the industry continues to evolve, wholesalers must adapt and prepare for future changes to remain successful.

Future - Photo by Tara Winstead

This chapter covers various topics such as understanding the evolution of the real estate industry, identifying future trends and challenges, preparing your business for future changes, staying ahead of the curve with technology and innovation, and contributing to the future of wholesale real estate investing.

17.1 Understanding the Evolution of the Real Estate Industry

The real estate industry has gone through various changes in recent years, including the **emergence of new technologies**, **changing consumer behavior**, and **evolving market conditions**. Understanding how the industry has evolved and the trends that have driven these changes can help wholesalers better anticipate future developments. For example, the rise of ***online real estate marketplaces*** and the growing use of ***virtual tours*** have transformed the way properties are bought and sold.

As wholesalers, understanding these trends and adapting to them can help to keep your business competitive and profitable.

17.2 Identifying Future Trends and Challenges

To stay ahead in the industry, wholesalers must keep abreast of the latest trends and challenges. This includes keeping an eye on changes in consumer behavior, market conditions, and the regulatory environment. For example, changes in **interest rates**, **local zoning laws**, and **economic conditions** can all impact the real estate market. Keeping up to date with these changes and anticipating how they may affect your business can help you to make more informed decisions and adjust your strategies accordingly.

17.3 Preparing Your Business for Future Changes

Wholesalers must be proactive in preparing their businesses for future changes. This includes developing **contingency plans** for different scenarios, such as changes in market conditions, economic downturns, or regulatory changes. It's also essential to keep up to date with the **latest technology and software solutions** to streamline operations and increase efficiency. Having a plan in place can help wholesalers to react quickly to changes and stay ahead of the competition.

17.4 Staying Ahead of the Curve with Technology and Innovation

Technology is rapidly transforming the real estate industry, and wholesalers must stay up to date with the latest tools and innovations to remain competitive. For example, using ***virtual reality technology*** to create immersive property tours, implementing ***chatbots*** for customer service, and leveraging ***artificial intelligence*** for market analysis and lead generation are all ways to stay ahead of the curve. By embracing **new technologies** and **innovative solutions**, wholesalers can improve their operations, reduce costs, and enhance customer experiences.

17.5 Contributing to the Future of Wholesale Real Estate Investing

As the real estate industry continues to evolve, wholesalers can play a role in shaping its future. This includes **sharing knowledge**, **experiences**, and **best practices** with others in the industry, as well as actively participating in industry associations and events. By contributing to the collective knowledge and resources of the industry, wholesalers can help to drive innovation, promote ethical business practices, and build a stronger, more sustainable future for wholesale real estate investing.

Conclusion

The chapter highlights the importance of staying ahead of the curve and preparing for the future in the fast-changing world of real estate. By understanding the evolution of the industry, identifying future trends and challenges, and embracing technology and innovation, wholesalers can adapt and thrive in this dynamic marketplace. Contributing to the future of the industry through collaboration and knowledge sharing can help to build a stronger, more resilient wholesale real estate investing community.

Chapter 18: Growing Your Real Estate Portfolio with Wholesaling

Wholesale real estate investing is not only a business in itself but can also be a valuable tool for building your real estate investment portfolio.

Portfolio - uncredited

In this chapter, we will explore how wholesaling can help you grow your real estate portfolio, and how you can identify and leverage investment opportunities through wholesaling.

18.1 Understanding the Relationship between Wholesaling and Investing

Wholesaling and investing are closely related in the real estate industry. As a wholesaler, you are essentially sourcing and identifying good deals that other investors may be interested in. By doing so, you are **building relationships** with potential buyers and gaining a deep understanding of the real estate market in your area. This knowledge can be invaluable when it comes to making future investment decisions.

18.2 Identifying Investment Opportunities Through Wholesaling

As a wholesaler, you are always on the lookout for good deals. By constantly analyzing the real estate market and building relationships with buyers and sellers, you may come across investment opportunities that you wouldn't have found otherwise. By leveraging your wholesaling business, you can identify potential investment properties and **add them to YOUR portfolio**.

18.3 Balancing Short-Term Wholesaling Deals with Long-Term Investing Goals

It's important to keep your long-term investing goals in mind when wholesaling. While it may be tempting to focus solely on short-term wholesaling deals, it's important to strike a balance between immediate profits and long-term investments. You may want to allocate a certain portion of your wholesaling profits towards **purchasing properties** for your own portfolio or investing in other long-term opportunities.

18.4 Scaling Your Investing Business through Wholesaling

Wholesaling can also help you scale your real estate investing business. By building relationships with other investors, you can potentially **partner** with them on future investments. Additionally, by identifying good deals through wholesaling, you can build a pipeline of properties for your investment business.

Conclusion

Wholesale real estate investing is not only a great way to generate income, but it can also be a valuable tool for building your real estate investment portfolio. By leveraging wholesaling to identify investment opportunities and reinvesting your profits, you can grow your portfolio and achieve your long-term investing goals.

Chapter 19: Wholesaling and Other Real Estate Investment Strategies

Real estate investing is a vast field, and there are various strategies available to investors.

Wholesaling is one of the most popular investment strategies, but it is not the only option.

Online Investing - Photo by Joshua Mayo

This chapter explores other real estate investment strategies that can ***complement*** or ***supplement*** wholesaling.

19.1 Understanding the Pros and Cons of Other Real Estate Investment Strategies

Real estate investors have many different investment strategies to choose from. Each strategy has its unique advantages and disadvantages, and it is essential to understand them before making investment decisions. Some common real estate investment strategies include:

- **Buy and hold:** This strategy involves purchasing properties with the intention of holding them for an extended period. The aim is to generate income through rent payments and appreciation over time.
- **Flipping:** This strategy involves purchasing properties that need repairs or renovations, making the necessary improvements, and then selling them quickly for a profit.
- **REITs:** Real Estate Investment Trusts (REITs) are companies that own and operate income-producing real estate properties. Investors can buy shares in these companies, and the dividends are paid out of the rental income generated by the properties.
- **Crowdfunding:** This strategy involves pooling funds from multiple investors to purchase real estate properties. The investors own a share of the property and receive a percentage of the rental income and appreciation.

It is essential to evaluate the pros and cons of each investment strategy to determine which one aligns with your financial goals, risk tolerance, and investment horizon.

19.2 Identifying Complementary Investment Strategies to Wholesaling

Wholesaling can be an excellent entry point for new investors looking to get started in real estate investing. However, as investors gain more experience and build their portfolios, they may want to consider other investment strategies that can **complement wholesaling.**

For example, an investor who is successful at wholesaling may consider **buying and holding** properties to generate long-term rental income. Alternatively, an investor who focuses on **flipping properties** may also wholesale properties that do not meet their investment criteria.

19.3 Diversifying Your Investment Portfolio with Different Strategies

Diversification is essential in any investment portfolio, including real estate. Having a mix of different investment strategies can help **mitigate risk** and **increase potential returns**.

Investors can diversify their real estate investment portfolios by combining different investment strategies, such as wholesaling, flipping, and REITs. By doing so, investors can spread their investments across different types of properties, geographic locations, and risk profiles.

19.4 Developing a Holistic Investment Approach

A holistic investment approach considers all aspects of an investor's financial goals, risk tolerance, and investment horizon. To develop a holistic investment approach, investors should consider their **short-term** and **long-term** financial goals, liquidity needs, and tax implications.

Wholesaling can be a useful tool for generating quick cash, but it should be part of a **broader investment strategy** that aligns with an investor's financial goals. For example, if an investor's goal is to generate long-term rental income, they may need to hold onto some of the properties they wholesale.

19.5 Knowing When to Pivot or Adjust Your Investment Strategy

Real estate investing is a dynamic industry, and market conditions can change quickly. Therefore, investors must be adaptable and willing to **pivot or adjust their investment strategies** when necessary.

For example, if the real estate market experiences a downturn, wholesalers may need to adjust their **pricing strategies** or focus on **different types of properties**. Alternatively, an investor who was successful at flipping properties may need to pivot to a buy-and-hold strategy during a market downturn.

Conclusion

In conclusion, wholesaling is a lucrative real estate investment strategy that can offer numerous benefits to investors. However, it is not the only investment strategy available, and it may not be suitable for everyone. Understanding the pros and cons of other investment strategies is crucial to building a well-diversified portfolio that can weather market changes and economic downturns. By identifying complementary investment strategies, investors can maximize their returns and minimize risks. Additionally, having a holistic investment approach that incorporates multiple strategies can provide a more stable foundation for long-term wealth-building. Knowing when to pivot or adjust your investment strategy is also essential for adapting to changes in the market and achieving continued success as a real estate investor.

Chapter 20: Taking Action and Getting Started with Wholesale Real Estate investing

In wholesale real estate investing, taking action is critical. Many aspiring wholesalers get stuck in a cycle of ***analysis paralysis***, where they endlessly research and analyze deals but never take action.

Action - Photo by Mason Kimbarovsky

This chapter aims to provide guidance for those looking to overcome this hurdle and take their first steps toward becoming a successful real estate wholesaler.

20.1 Overcoming Analysis Paralysis and Taking Action

Analysis paralysis is a common problem that affects many new real estate wholesalers. This is the state where an individual is overwhelmed with information, and **cannot decide** on the best course of action. To overcome analysis paralysis, it is essential to establish a **clear plan** and take **small steps** toward achieving that plan. One way to get started is by setting small, achievable goals that are measurable and time-bound. These goals can help individuals break down their overall objectives into manageable chunks and keep them motivated to keep taking action.

20.2 Identifying Your First Wholesaling Deal

Identifying the right deal is critical to the success of a wholesale real estate investing business. To find the right deal, wholesalers must understand their target market, research the market, and network with potential buyers and sellers. It is also essential to have a clear understanding of what makes a good deal, including factors such as the potential profit, the location, the condition of the property, and the level of demand in the market.

20.3 Overcoming the Fear of Failure

Fear of failure is a common barrier that many aspiring wholesalers must overcome. To overcome this fear, it is important to **focus on the long-term benefits** of taking action and to recognize that failure is often an inevitable part of the learning process. It is also important to seek support from a mentor or a supportive community of peers who can provide guidance and encouragement.

20.4 Celebrating Your Successes and Milestones

Celebrating successes and milestones is critical for maintaining motivation and building confidence in the wholesale real estate investing business. It is essential to take the time to **reflect on each success,** no matter how small, and to recognize the effort and hard work that went into achieving that success. This can be as simple as taking time to appreciate each closed deal or setting up a system for tracking progress toward larger goals.

20.5 Continuing to Learn and Grow as a Real Estate Wholesaler

The real estate market is constantly evolving, and as a wholesaler, it is essential to keep learning and growing to stay ahead of the curve. This may involve attending **industry conferences**, reading **industry publications**, taking **courses or workshops**, and **networking** with peers in the industry. It is also important to regularly evaluate the wholesaling business model and look for ways to improve and innovate.

Conclusion

Wholesale real estate investing can be a highly rewarding and lucrative business for those who are willing to take action and commit to ongoing learning and growth. By overcoming analysis paralysis, identifying the right deal, overcoming the fear of failure, celebrating successes and milestones, and continuing to learn and grow, aspiring wholesalers can establish a strong foundation for success in this exciting and dynamic industry.

Chapter 21: Celebrating Your Wholesaling Successes

Wholesaling can be a challenging business, with many obstacles and setbacks along the way. However, it's important to take time to celebrate your successes and accomplishments. Doing so can help you ***stay motivated***, ***build confidence***, and ***inspire others*** in the industry.

Celebration - Photo by Al Elmes

In this chapter, we'll explore different ways to celebrate your wholesaling successes.

21.1 Reflecting on Your Accomplishments and Progress

One of the best ways to celebrate your wholesaling successes is to take time to reflect on your accomplishments and progress. Look back at your journey and consider all the hard work, dedication, and persistence that got you to where you are today. Celebrate the **small milestones**, as well as the **big successes**. Reflecting on your achievements can help you appreciate how far you've come and give you the motivation to keep pushing forward.

21.2 Acknowledging the Hard Work and Dedication Required for Wholesaling

Wholesaling is not an easy business. It requires hard work, dedication, and a willingness to take risks. When you celebrate your wholesaling successes, take time to acknowledge all the **effort and energy** you put into your business. Recognize the late nights, early mornings, and sacrifices you made to get to where you are today. By acknowledging the hard work required for success, you can build a deeper sense of pride and accomplishment.

21.3 Sharing Your Successes with Others in the Industry

Wholesaling is a tight-knit community, and celebrating your successes can inspire others in the industry. **Share your accomplishments** with other wholesalers, real estate agents, and investors. By sharing your successes, you can show others what's possible and inspire them to keep pushing forward. Additionally, sharing your successes can help you build valuable relationships in the industry and open up new opportunities.

21.4 Recognizing and Thanking Your Team and Supporters

Wholesaling is not a one-person job. It takes a team of people to make a successful wholesaling business. When you celebrate your successes, make sure to **recognize and thank your team and supporters**. This can include your virtual ***assistant***, ***marketing team***, ***real estate agent***, and ***investors***. By showing gratitude, you can build stronger relationships and create a supportive network that can help you achieve even greater success in the future.

21.5 Continuing to Strive for Growth and Improvement in Your Wholesaling Business

While it's important to celebrate your wholesaling successes, it's also essential to keep pushing forward and striving for growth and improvement. Use your successes as motivation to set **new goals** and take your wholesaling business to the **next level**. Continuously seek out new opportunities to learn and grow, and never be satisfied with the status quo. Celebrating your successes is just one step on the journey to becoming a successful wholesaler.

Conclusion

In conclusion, celebrating your wholesaling successes is an essential part of building a successful wholesaling business. It can help you stay motivated, build confidence, and inspire others in the industry. By reflecting on your accomplishments, acknowledging the hard work required for success, sharing your successes with others, recognizing and thanking your team and supporters, and continuing to strive for growth and improvement, you can create a thriving wholesaling business and achieve your goals.

Chapter 22: Understanding Real Estate Market Cycles for Wholesaling Real Estate Investing

Real estate market cycles are a crucial aspect of the real estate industry that can have a significant impact on the value and demand for properties. As a result, understanding market cycles is essential for real estate investors, including wholesalers, as it can inform investment decisions and strategies.

Market Cycles - Photo by Burak The Weekender

In this chapter, we will explore what real estate market cycles are, how they affect wholesaling, and how to identify market trends and indicators. We will also discuss the importance of timing investments based on market cycles and navigating challenges during market downturns.

22.1 What Are Real Estate Market Cycles?

Real estate market cycles refer to the **pattern of ups and downs** in the real estate market, driven by various ***economic***, ***demographic***, and ***political factors***. These cycles can have a significant impact on the value and demand for properties, as well as the overall health of the real estate industry. Understanding market cycles is important for real estate investors, including wholesalers, as it can inform investment decisions and strategies.

22.2 How Market Cycles Affect Wholesaling

Market cycles can have a significant impact on wholesalers, as the profitability and demand for their services are closely tied to the state of the market. During a **hot market** with high demand and low inventory, wholesalers may have an easier time finding buyers for their properties, but may also face more competition from other investors. Conversely, during a **downturn or recession**, wholesalers may struggle to find buyers and may need to adjust their strategies to account for the changing market conditions.

22.3 Identifying Market Trends and Indicators

To understand market cycles and make informed investment decisions, wholesalers should pay attention to a range of market trends and indicators, including factors such as **interest rates**, **housing inventory**, **employment rates**, **population growth**, and more. Additionally, analyzing historical market data and tracking market predictions and forecasts can provide valuable insights into current and future market conditions.

22.4 Timing Your Investments Based on Market Cycles

Timing is a key factor in wholesaling success, and wholesalers should aim to time their investments to take advantage of **favorable market conditions**. This may be knowing that their investors are selling more properties during a hot market when prices are high, or buying properties during a downturn when prices are lower and demand is weaker. Additionally, wholesalers should be prepared to adjust their strategies as market conditions change to optimize their profitability and minimize risk.

22.5 Navigating Challenges During Market Downturns

Market downturns and recessions can pose significant challenges for wholesalers, as **demand for properties may decrease**, and **competition may increase**. During these times, wholesalers may need to be more creative in their marketing and financing strategies, work more closely with motivated sellers to identify potential deals, and potentially adjust their pricing and fee structures to remain competitive. Additionally, having a solid understanding of market trends and conditions can help wholesalers navigate challenges and minimize risk during market downturns.

Conclusion

In conclusion, understanding real estate market cycles is essential for wholesalers to succeed in the real estate industry. By paying attention to market trends and indicators, wholesalers can make informed investment decisions and adjust their strategies to optimize their profitability and minimize risk. Additionally, timing investments based on market cycles can help wholesalers take advantage of favorable market conditions and navigate challenges during market downturns. Overall, a solid understanding of real estate market cycles is crucial for wholesalers to thrive in the ever-changing real estate industry.

Chapter 23: Managing Risks in Wholesaling Real Estate Investing

Wholesaling real estate investing can be a lucrative business, but it also comes with its fair share of risks.

Risk - Photo by Anthony Fomin

In this chapter, we will explore the potential risks and challenges that wholesalers may face and discuss strategies for managing them. From conducting due diligence to securing adequate insurance and developing a risk management plan, we will provide valuable insights for wholesalers looking to protect their investments and minimize their exposure to risk.

23.1 Understanding the Risks Involved in Wholesaling

Wholesale real estate investing can be a high-risk, high-reward venture, and it is important for wholesalers to understand the potential risks and challenges they may face. These may include **market fluctuations**,

legal and regulatory issues, and **unforeseen expenses** or **complications** during the buying and selling process.

23.2 Conducting Due Diligence

To manage these risks, wholesalers should conduct thorough due diligence on each property they consider making an offer on. This may involve conducting **property inspections**, **reviewing legal and financial documents**, and **assessing potential repair or maintenance costs.**

23.3 Using Contingency Clauses

Contingency clauses are contractual provisions that allow buyers and sellers to back out of a deal under specific circumstances, such as a **failed inspection** or **financing issue**. Including contingency clauses in purchase agreements can help wholesalers mitigate risk and protect their investments.

23.4 Securing Adequate Insurance

Wholesalers should also ensure they have adequate insurance coverage to protect against **unforeseen events** such as ***liability claims***, or ***legal disputes***. This may involve obtaining general **liability insurance** and **errors and omissions insurance**.

23.5 Developing a Risk Management Plan

Finally, wholesalers should develop a comprehensive **risk management plan** that addresses potential **risks and challenges** and outlines strategies for mitigating them. This may involve identifying potential risks, assessing their likelihood and impact, and developing contingency plans and mitigation strategies to address each risk as it arises.

Conclusion

In conclusion, managing risks in wholesaling real estate investing is essential for success in this industry. By understanding the potential risks and challenges, conducting thorough due diligence, using contingency clauses, securing adequate insurance, and developing a comprehensive risk management plan, wholesalers can protect their investments and minimize their exposure to risk. With these strategies in place, wholesalers can focus on maximizing their profits and achieving their business goals.

Chapter 24: Legal and Ethical Considerations in Wholesaling Real Estate Investing

Wholesaling real estate investing can be a lucrative business, but it also comes with a range of legal and ethical considerations that must be taken into account. From compliance with laws and regulations to ethical business practices and proper disclosures, wholesalers must navigate a complex landscape to ensure they are operating within the bounds of the law and maintaining ethical standards.

Legal - Photo by August de Richelieu

In this chapter, we will explore the key legal and ethical considerations that wholesalers must be aware of in order to succeed in this industry.

24.1 Understanding Legal and Ethical Considerations in Wholesaling

Wholesaling real estate investing involves a number of legal and ethical considerations, including compliance with **federal, state, and local laws**, **ethical business practices**, and **proper disclosures** to buyers and sellers.

24.2 Compliance with laws and regulations

Wholesalers must comply with a range of laws and regulations governing real estate investing, including **licensing requirements**, **anti-fraud laws**, **fair housing laws**, and **zoning and land use regulations.** Failure to comply with these laws can result in legal and financial consequences.

24.3 Ethical business practices

In addition to legal requirements, wholesalers must also adhere to ethical business practices, such as **honesty** and **transparency** in dealing with buyers and sellers, **fair pricing**, and **full disclosure** of any potential conflicts of interest.

24.4 Disclosures to Buyers and Sellers

Wholesalers must also provide buyers and sellers with **full disclosure** of any relevant information about the property, including any defects or issues that may affect its value or marketability. Failure to provide accurate and complete disclosures can result in legal and financial liability.

24.5 Seeking professional advice and guidance

To ensure compliance with legal and ethical requirements, wholesalers should seek the guidance of experienced real estate **attorneys**,

accountants, and other professionals who can provide advice and assistance in navigating the complex legal and regulatory landscape of real estate investing.

Conclusion

In conclusion, wholesaling real estate investing requires a deep understanding of the legal and ethical considerations that come with this business. Compliance with laws and regulations, ethical business practices, and proper disclosures are all essential components of a successful wholesaling operation. By seeking the guidance of experienced professionals and staying up-to-date on the latest legal and regulatory developments, wholesalers can ensure they are operating within the bounds of the law and maintaining ethical standards, while also maximizing their profits and building a successful business.

Chapter 25: Best Practices for Wholesaling Real Estate Investing

Wholesaling real estate investing can be a lucrative business, but it requires a deep understanding of the market and a commitment to best practices.

Practice - Photo by Sigmund

In this chapter, we will explore the key strategies for success in wholesaling real estate investing, including understanding your target market, developing strong relationships with buyers and sellers, prioritizing quality over quantity, staying up-to-date with industry trends and best practices, and investing in your own education and development.

25.1 Understanding your target market

Understanding your **target market** is essential for success in wholesaling real estate investing. By identifying the ***needs***, ***preferences***, and ***behaviors*** of your customers, you can tailor your marketing and sales strategies to better meet their needs and achieve greater success.

25.2 Developing strong relationships with buyers and sellers

Developing **strong relationships** with buyers and sellers is also important in wholesaling real estate investing. By building ***trust***, ***communicating*** effectively, and providing high-quality ***service***, you can establish long-term relationships that can help you generate more leads and achieve greater profitability.

25.3 Prioritizing Quality over Quantity

Prioritizing quality over quantity is another best practice in wholesaling real estate investing. Rather than focusing on volume and quantity, it is important to **focus on quality** and ensuring that you are providing high-quality service and value to your customers.

25.4 Staying up-to-date with industry trends and best practices

Staying up-to-date with industry trends and best practices is essential for success in wholesaling real estate investing. By **staying informed** about the latest developments, you can remain competitive in the market and identify new opportunities for growth and success.

25.5 Investing in your own education and development

Finally, investing in your own education and development is essential for success in wholesaling real estate investing. By **continuously learning** and developing **new skills** and **knowledge**, you can improve your performance, expand your capabilities, and achieve greater success in your business.

Conclusion

In conclusion, wholesaling real estate investing requires a combination of knowledge, skill, and dedication to best practices. By understanding your target market, building strong relationships, prioritizing quality, staying up-to-date with industry trends, and investing in your own education and development, you can achieve greater success in your business. With these strategies in mind, you can navigate the challenges of the market and build a thriving wholesaling real estate investing business.

Chapter 26: Conclusion

26.1 Recap of Key Points

As we come to the end of this guide, it's important to recap the key points that we have covered in our discussion of wholesaling real estate investing.

The End - Photo by geralt

We have explored the **definition of wholesaling**, the **process involved** in this type of investing, the **pros and cons of wholesaling**, and the **common mistakes** that investors should avoid.

We have learned that wholesaling involves **finding motivated sellers**, **negotiating** with the owners, and then **assigning the contract** to a buyer who will take over the property. This process can be lucrative, but it requires a lot of hard work and dedication.

We have also discussed the **advantages and disadvantages** of wholesaling. On the one hand, it can be a quick way to make money without having to invest a lot of capital. On the other hand, it can be a competitive field, and there are risks involved in dealing with distressed properties.

Finally, we have looked at some of the **common mistakes** that investors make when wholesaling. These include not doing enough research, not building relationships with buyers and sellers, and not having a solid understanding of the market.

26.2 Importance of Education and Research

One of the key takeaways from this guide is the importance of education and research in the world of wholesaling real estate investing. It's crucial to **stay informed** about the latest trends and developments in the market, as well as to **conduct thorough research** on potential markets.

By continuing to educate yourself and stay up-to-date on the latest industry news, you can make more informed investment decisions and increase your chances of success in this competitive field.

26.3 Final Thoughts

In conclusion, wholesaling real estate investing can be a lucrative and rewarding endeavor, but it requires **hard work**, **dedication**, and a **willingness to learn and adapt**. By following the tips and strategies outlined in this guide, you can increase your chances of success in this competitive field.

Remember to always do your research, build strong relationships with buyers and sellers, and stay informed about the latest trends and developments in the market. With these tools and a commitment to hard work, you can achieve your goals and find success in the world of wholesaling real estate investing.

Good luck.

Check out WWW.JIMPELLERIN.COM[1] for more articles

on Real Estate Investing.

1. http://WWW.JIMPELLERIN.COM

Appendix A: The Step-by-Step Guide to Wholesale Real Estate Investing

The Ultimate Wholesale Real Estate Investing Strategy is a unique Strategy that helps wholesalers complete more wholesale deals without spending a lot of time looking for motivated sellers, negotiating the best deals, or finding cash buyers to complete more wholesale deals. The following is a step-by-step guide to wholesale real estate investing and are the recommended steps you should follow:

1. **Develop a Business Plan:** Developing a solid business plan is an important first step when starting a wholesale real estate business. It should include a clear vision, mission statement, goals, target market, marketing strategy, budget, and revenue projections. A well-crafted business plan will help you stay focused and organized, as well as provide a roadmap for

achieving your business objectives.

2. **Research the Market:** In order to succeed in the wholesale real estate business, it's important to have a deep understanding of the market where you plan to operate your business. This includes understanding the types of properties that are in demand, the areas that are most attractive to buyers and investors, and the current market trends. You should also research the competition to identify what they're doing well and what areas they may be overlooking.
3. **Build a Network:** Building a strong network of real estate agents, brokers, investors, attorneys, and other professionals in the industry is crucial for success in the wholesale real estate business. Attend networking events, join local real estate associations, and use social media to connect with potential partners and clients. Having a strong network can provide you with valuable insights, and access to new opportunities, and help you build trust with potential clients.
4. **Build a Buyer's List:** In addition to identifying potential sellers, you'll also need to build a list of potential buyers who are interested in purchasing wholesale properties. This list should include investors, rehabbers, and other real estate professionals who are looking for good deals. Building a strong buyer's list takes time and effort, but it's essential for success in the wholesale real estate business.
5. **Find Motivated Sellers:** A successful wholesale real estate business requires motivated sellers and a comprehensive marketing plan that includes a variety of tactics to reach sellers. Direct mail, email campaigns, social media marketing, and other tactics can be used to attract motivated sellers who are willing to sell their properties at a discount. Your marketing strategy should be tailored to your target market and budget.

6. **Analyze Properties:** Once you've identified potential properties to purchase, it's important to conduct thorough due diligence to ensure that they're a good investment opportunity. This includes researching the property's condition, location, and potential for profitability. You may also want to work with a real estate agent or inspector to evaluate the property.
7. **Negotiate Deals:** The key to success in the wholesale real estate business is being able to negotiate deals with motivated sellers to purchase properties below market value. Your networking skills and market knowledge will be essential in identifying potential sellers and negotiating favorable terms.
8. **Market Properties:** Once you have acquired a property, you'll need to market it to potential buyers. This involves highlighting the benefits of each property and providing detailed information about its condition, location, and potential for profitability. Using effective marketing tactics such as targeted email campaigns, social media advertising, and open houses can help you reach potential buyers and close deals quickly.
9. **Manage Contracts:** Once you have a buyer for a property, it's important to manage the closing process to ensure that all parties are meeting their obligations. This includes working with a reputable title company or attorney to manage the closing process and ensuring that all necessary documents are signed and filed appropriately.
10. **Repeat:** Finally, it's important to repeat the process by identifying new properties, negotiating deals, and marketing to potential buyers. Over time, you'll build a successful wholesale real estate business that provides you with a steady stream of income. However, it's important to stay informed about the latest market trends and continue building your

network to stay competitive in the industry.

Step 1 - Develop a Business Plan

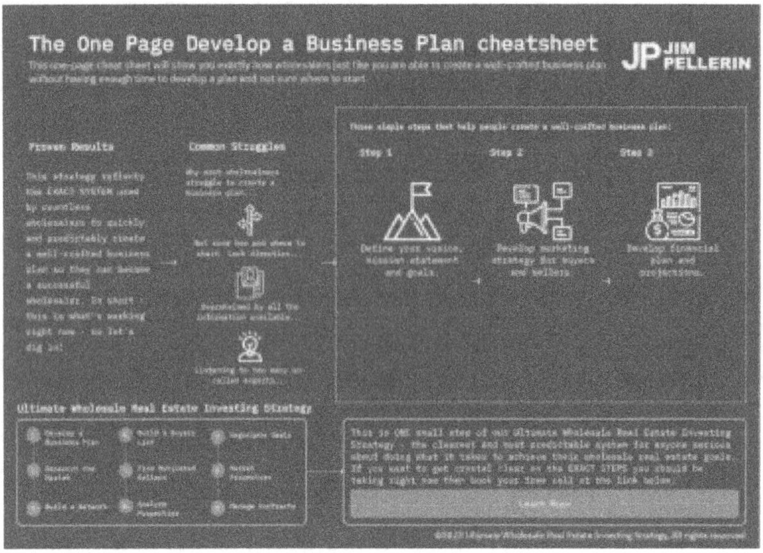

Developing a solid business plan is crucial when starting any business, including a wholesale real estate business. A well-crafted business plan can serve as a roadmap for achieving your business objectives and help you stay organized and focused. Here are some key elements to consider when developing a business plan for your wholesale real estate business:

1. **Executive Summary:** This section should provide an overview of your business, including your ***mission statement***, ***vision***, and ***goals***.
2. **Company Description:** Describe your business in more detail, including the type of properties you plan to wholesale, the geographic area you plan to serve, and any unique selling points that differentiate you from competitors.
3. **Market Analysis:** This section should provide a high-level

analysis of the real estate market in your target area, including current market trends, the demand for wholesale properties, and any potential challenges or obstacles.

4. **Marketing Strategy:** Outline your marketing strategy and tactics, including how you plan to reach potential sellers and buyers, what channels you will use, and any promotional activities you plan to undertake.
5. **Financial Projections:** Create financial projections based on your revenue expectations, operating expenses, and start-up costs. This should include cash flow projections, profit and loss statements, and balance sheets.
6. **Management Team:** Describe the management team that will be responsible for running the business, including their backgrounds, skills, and experience.
7. **Legal Structure:** Determine the legal structure of your business, such as whether you will operate as a sole proprietorship, partnership, LLC, or corporation.
8. **Funding Needs:** If you plan to seek funding to start or grow your business, outline your funding needs and how you plan to use the funds.
9. **Risk Management:** Identify potential risks and challenges that may impact your business and create a plan for how you will mitigate these risks.
10. **Exit Strategy:** Determine your exit strategy, such as whether you plan to sell the business, transfer ownership to a family member, or retire.

Developing a business plan can be time-consuming, but it's an essential step in starting a wholesale real estate business. A well-crafted plan will help you clarify your business goals, assess the market, and create a roadmap for success. It will also provide a framework for measuring your progress and making adjustments as needed.

Step 2 - Research the Market

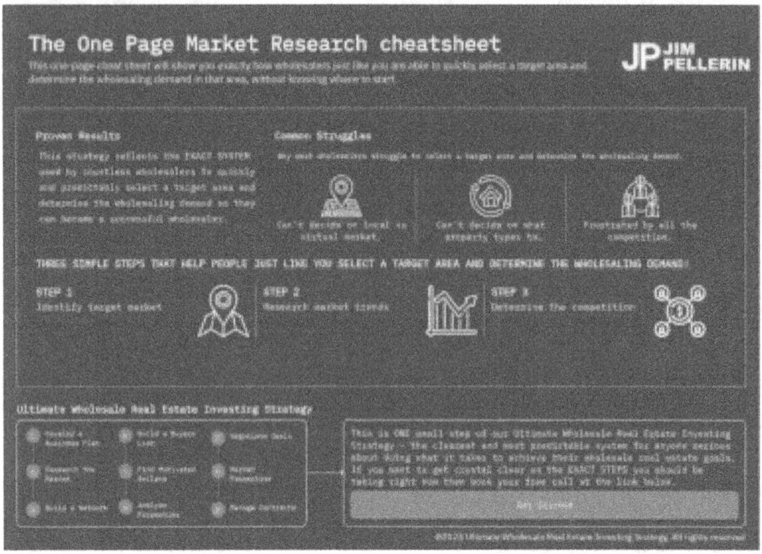

Researching the market is an important step when starting a wholesale real estate business. It will help you understand the demand for properties in your target area and determine what types of properties are in demand. Here are some steps to take when researching the market for your wholesale real estate business:

1. **Identify Your Target Area:** Start by identifying the geographic area in which you plan to operate. This could be a city, county, or region. Once you have identified your target area, research the real estate market in that area.
2. **Analyze Real Estate Trends:** Use real estate data and analytics tools to analyze the trends in your target area. This could include data on home prices, inventory levels, days on market, and other key indicators. Look for patterns and trends in the data that may indicate whether the market is growing or contracting, and identify any areas where there may be opportunities to find wholesale properties.

3. **Research Demographics:** Study the demographics of the area to understand who your potential buyers and sellers may be. Look for information on population trends, income levels, education levels, and other relevant factors that could impact the real estate market.
4. **Identify Local Real Estate Agents:** Get in touch with local real estate agents who can provide valuable insights into the market. Ask them about their experience working with wholesale real estate investors and find out what types of properties are in demand in the area.
5. **Attend Real Estate Networking Events:** Attend real estate networking events in your area to meet other investors, agents, and industry professionals. These events can be a great way to learn about the local market and make connections with potential partners and clients.
6. **Research Local Laws and Regulations:** Be sure to research local laws and regulations related to wholesale real estate investing in your target area. This could include zoning laws, building codes, and other regulations that could impact your ability to wholesale properties.

By researching the market, you can gain a better understanding of the demand for wholesale properties in your target area and identify opportunities to find properties that meet the needs of potential buyers. This information will be critical as you develop your marketing and acquisition strategies.

Step 3 - Build a Network

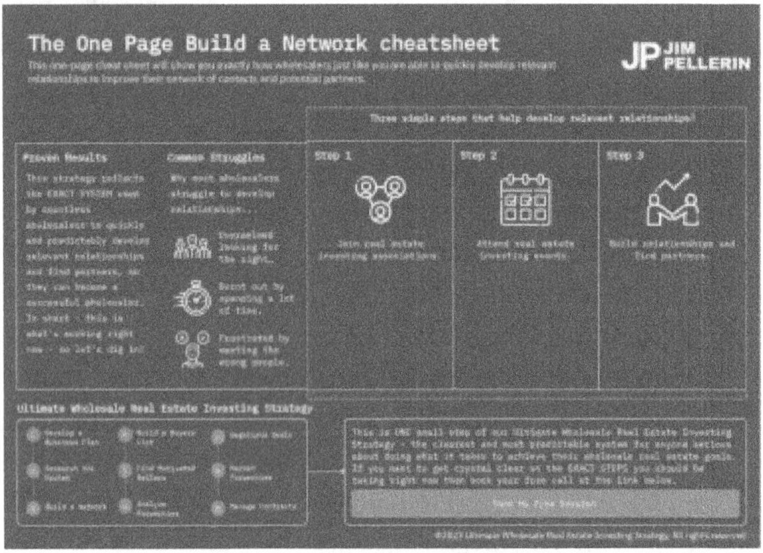

Building a network of contacts is an essential step when starting a wholesale real estate business. A strong network can help you find potential buyers and sellers, and build your reputation in the industry. Here are some steps you can take to build your network:

1. **Join Real Estate Associations:** Join local and national real estate investors associations, such as the local ***Real Estate Investors Association***. These associations can provide valuable networking opportunities and resources for real estate professionals.
2. **Attend Real Estate Conferences:** Attend real estate conferences and seminars to meet other investors, brokers, and industry professionals. These events can be a great way to learn about the latest trends and best practices in the industry.
3. **Network Online:** Use social media and online forums to connect with other real estate professionals. Join ***LinkedIn***

and ***Facebook*** groups and participate in online discussions related to real estate investing.

4. **Partner with Real Estate Agents:** Build relationships with real estate agents who can help you find potential buyers and sellers. Offer to refer clients to them in exchange for referrals to wholesale properties.
5. **Build Relationships with Wholesalers:** Network with other wholesale real estate investors to share leads and build relationships for potential joint ventures. Join local wholesaling groups or start your own mastermind group.
6. **Attend Local Real Estate Meetups:** Attend local real estate meetups and networking events to connect with other investors, agents, and industry professionals in your area.

Building a strong network of contacts can take time and effort, but it is essential for success in the wholesale real estate business. By connecting with other professionals in the industry, you can build your reputation, find potential buyers and sellers, and stay up to date on the latest trends and best practices in the industry.

Step 4 - Build a Buyers List

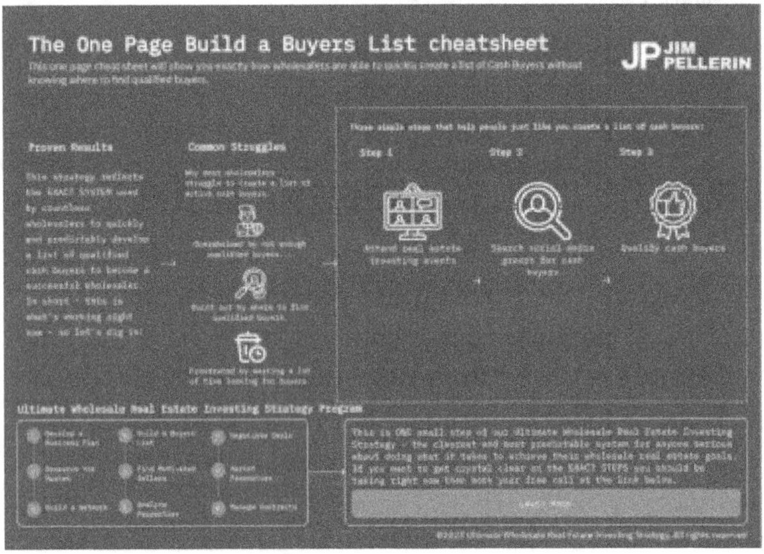

Building a buyer's list is an essential step in the wholesale real estate business. A buyer's list is a database of potential buyers who are interested in purchasing properties from you. Here are some steps you can take to build a buyer's list:

1. **Attend Real Estate Meetups:** Attend real estate meetups and networking events to meet potential buyers. Bring business cards and be prepared to share information about your wholesale real estate business and the properties you have available.
2. **Use Social Media:** Use social media platforms like ***Facebook Groups***, ***LinkedIn***, and ***Twitter*** to connect with potential buyers. Post about the properties you have available and share industry news and insights to build your brand and attract potential buyers.
3. **Place Ads:** Place ads on Craigslist, Facebook Marketplace, and other online platforms to attract potential buyers. Make

sure to include details about the properties you have available, the asking price, and any other relevant information.

4. **Reach Out to Real Estate Agents:** Real estate agents often work with buyers who are interested in purchasing investment properties. Reach out to local agents and let them know about the properties you have available. Offer them a commission for bringing a buyer to the table.
5. **Attend Real Estate Auctions:** Attend real estate auctions to meet potential buyers who are interested in purchasing investment properties. Bring business cards and be prepared to share information about your wholesale real estate business.
6. **Use Email Marketing:** Use email marketing to keep in touch with potential buyers. Collect email addresses through your website, social media groups, or networking events, and send regular newsletters or updates about properties you have available.

Building a buyer's list takes time and effort, but it is essential for success in the wholesale real estate business. By attending networking events, using social media, placing ads, reaching out to real estate agents, attending auctions, hosting open houses, and using email marketing, you can build a strong buyer's list and generate leads for your wholesale real estate business.

Step 5 - Find Motivated Sellers

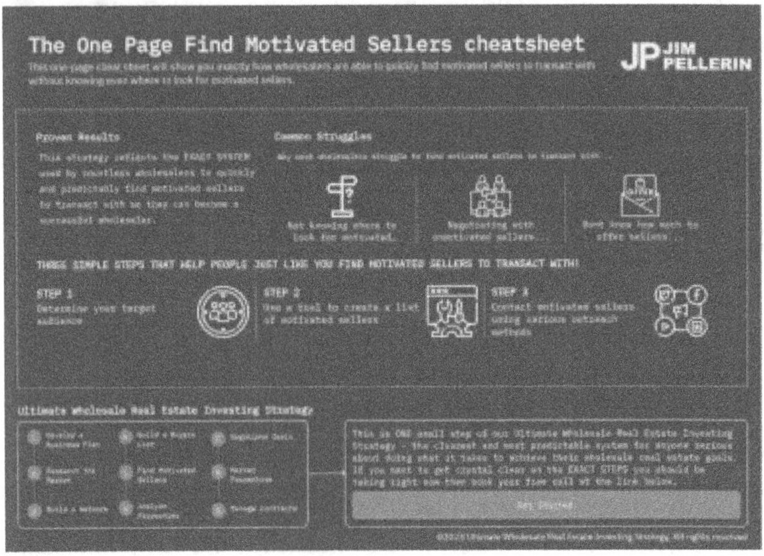

Finding motivated sellers is a crucial step in starting a successful wholesale real estate business. A well-crafted marketing plan can help you reach potential sellers, generate leads, and build your brand in the industry. Here are some steps you can take to create a marketing plan for motivated sellers for your wholesale real estate business:

1. **Identify Your Target Audience:** The first step in creating a marketing plan is to identify your target audience. Who are you trying to reach? Are you targeting foreclosures, vacant homeowners, or disgruntled landlords? Once you have identified your target audience, you can create a message that will resonate with them.
2. **Develop Your Brand:** Develop a brand that is professional and memorable. This includes creating a logo, website, business cards, and other marketing materials that represent your business.
3. **Create a Website:** A website is an essential tool for any

business, including a wholesale real estate business. Your website should be easy to navigate, provide information about your services, and include contact information.

4. **Use Social Media:** Social media platforms such as ***Facebook***, ***Twitter***, and ***Instagram*** can be great tools for marketing your wholesale real estate business. Use social media to share information about your business, post pictures of past properties, and engage with potential sellers.
5. **Develop Content:** Creating content such as blog posts, videos, and infographics can help establish your business as an authority in the industry. Share your content on your website and social media channels to reach a wider audience.
6. **Use Direct Mail:** Direct mail campaigns can be a cost-effective way to reach potentially motivated sellers. Consider sending postcards or letters to targeted lists of homeowners or investors.
7. **Offer Referral Incentives:** Offer referral incentives to encourage satisfied clients and business partners to refer others to your wholesale real estate business.
8. **Monitor Your Results:** Keep track of your marketing efforts and their results. This will allow you to determine what is working and what needs improvement. Use this information to adjust your marketing plan and continue to improve your efforts.

Creating a marketing plan for your wholesale real estate business takes time and effort, but it is essential for reaching motivated sellers and building your brand in the industry. By identifying your target audience, developing your brand, and using a variety of marketing tactics, you can generate leads and build your business.

Step 6 - Analyze Properties

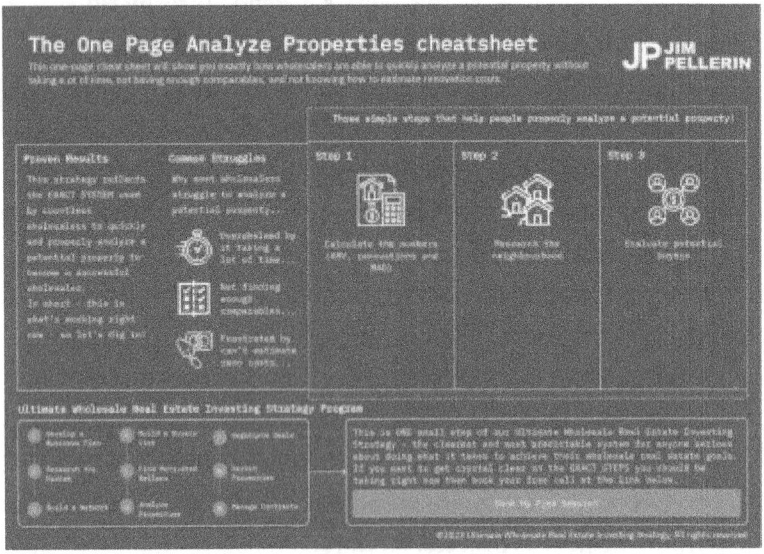

Analyzing properties is a crucial step in the wholesale real estate business. It is important to carefully evaluate each property you are considering for purchase to ensure that it is a good investment. Here are some steps you can take to analyze properties:

1. **Determine the After Repair Value (ARV):** The ARV is the estimated value of the property after it has been renovated or repaired. This is an essential factor in determining whether a property is a good investment.
2. **Evaluate the Repairs Needed:** Determine what repairs are needed for the property and estimate the cost of those repairs. This will help you determine whether the property is a good investment and whether you can make a profit on the deal.
3. **Research the Neighborhood:** Research the neighborhood where the property is located. Look at recent sales of similar properties, crime rates, schools, and other factors that could

affect the value of the property.

4. **Determine the Purchase Price:** Based on the ARV and the cost of repairs, determine the maximum allowable offer (MAO) you are willing to pay for the property. This should leave room for profit when you assign the property to a buyer.
5. **Evaluate Potential Buyers:** Consider the types of buyers who may be interested in the property. This can help you determine how much profit you can make on the deal and how quickly you can sell the property.
6. **Calculate the Expected Profit:** Based on the ARV, the cost of repairs, and the potential buyers, calculate the expected profit on the deal. This will help you determine whether the property is a good investment and whether you should move forward to the next step.

Analyzing properties takes time and effort, but it is essential for success in the wholesale real estate business. By carefully evaluating each property you are considering for purchase, you can ensure that it is a good investment and that you can make a profit on the deal.

Step 7 - Negotiate Deals

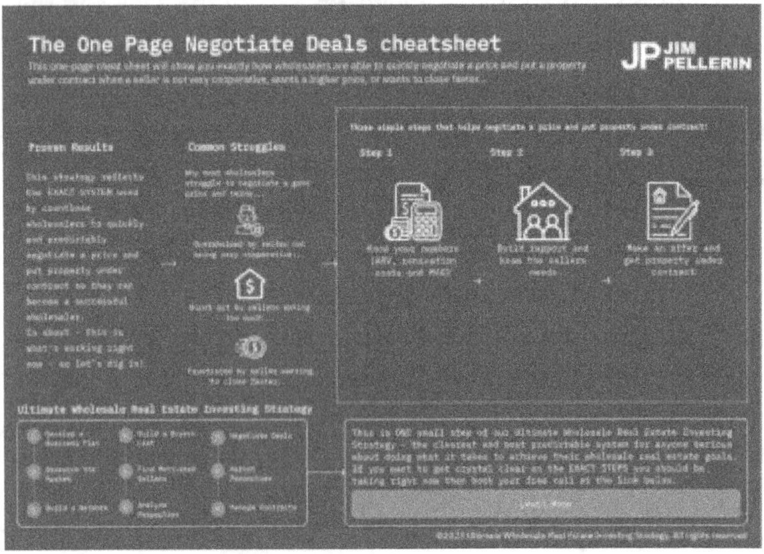

Negotiating deals is a critical skill for success in the wholesale real estate business. As a wholesaler, you are essentially a middleman, connecting motivated sellers with potential buyers. Here are some steps you can take to negotiate deals effectively:

1. **Know Your Numbers:** It is essential to know your numbers and have a clear understanding of what a property is worth, what repairs are needed, and what the after-repair value (ARV) is. This will give you leverage in negotiations and help you determine what price you can offer (MAO) to the seller while still leaving room for profit.
2. **Build Rapport:** Building a good relationship with the seller can help you negotiate a better deal. Take the time to get to know the seller and build rapport. Ask about their situation and why they are selling the property. This can help you understand their motivations and negotiate a better deal.
3. **Understand the Seller's Needs:** Understanding the seller's

needs is crucial for negotiating a successful deal. Determine what is most important to the seller - price, speed of sale, or another factor - and use this information to negotiate a deal that works for both parties.

4. **Make an Offer:** Once you have a clear understanding of the property and the seller's needs, make an offer. Start with a low offer and be prepared to negotiate. Remember that your goal is to get a good deal that leaves profit for the potential buyer.
5. **Be Flexible:** Negotiations can be complex and involve a lot of back and forth. Be flexible and willing to compromise to reach a deal that works for both parties.
6. **Use Creative Financing:** In some cases, creative financing can help you close a deal. Consider asking for seller financing, lease options, or other creative financing options to make the deal more attractive to the ultimate buyer.
7. **Place Property Under Contract:** If you are able to negotiate a price and terms that are favorable to you and a potential buyer, then place the property under contract. This means executing a purchase and sale agreement between you and the seller.

Negotiating deals takes time, patience, and skill. By building rapport with the seller, understanding their needs, and being flexible in negotiations, you can negotiate successful deals and build a successful wholesale real estate business.

Step 8 - Market Properties

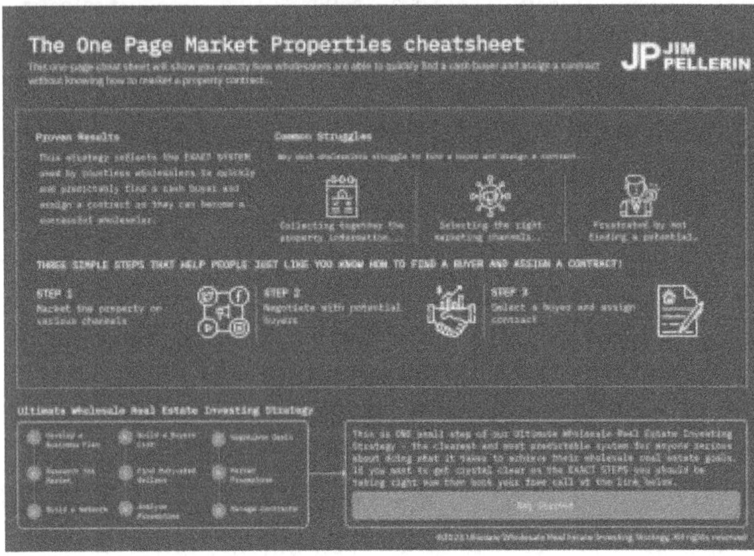

Marketing properties is a crucial step in the wholesale real estate business. Your ability to market properties effectively will impact the success of your wholesale deals. Here are some steps you can take to market properties effectively:

1. **Take High-Quality Photos:** High-quality photos are essential for marketing properties. Take clear and well-lit photos of the property's exterior and interior, including all the rooms and any unique features.
2. **Create a Property Description:** Write a clear and concise property description that highlights the property's key features and benefits. Include the property's location, size, number of bedrooms and bathrooms, and any special features, such as a pool, garage, or outdoor space.
3. **Use Online Listings:** Use online listings such as ***Craigslist*** and ***Facebook Marketplace*** to market your contract. Make sure to include high-quality photos and a detailed property

description.

4. **Reach Out to Your Buyer's List:** Reach out to your buyer's list and let them know about the property you have available. Provide them with the property description and photos, and invite them to schedule a showing.
5. **Use Social Media:** Use social media platforms like ***Facebook Groups***, ***Twitter***, and ***LinkedIn*** to market your contract. Share the property description and photos, and encourage your followers to share the information with their networks.
6. **Host an Open House:** Hosting an open house is a great way to generate interest in the property. Advertise the open house on social media and through online listings, and make sure the property is clean and staged for the event.
7. **Assign Contract:** Find the perfect buyer and assign the contract to that buyer.

Marketing properties takes time and effort, but it is an essential step in the wholesale real estate business. By taking high-quality photos, creating a property description and marketing flyer, using online listings and social media, reaching out to your buyer's list, and hosting an open house, you can market your properties effectively and generate leads for your wholesale real estate business.

Step 9 - Manage Contracts

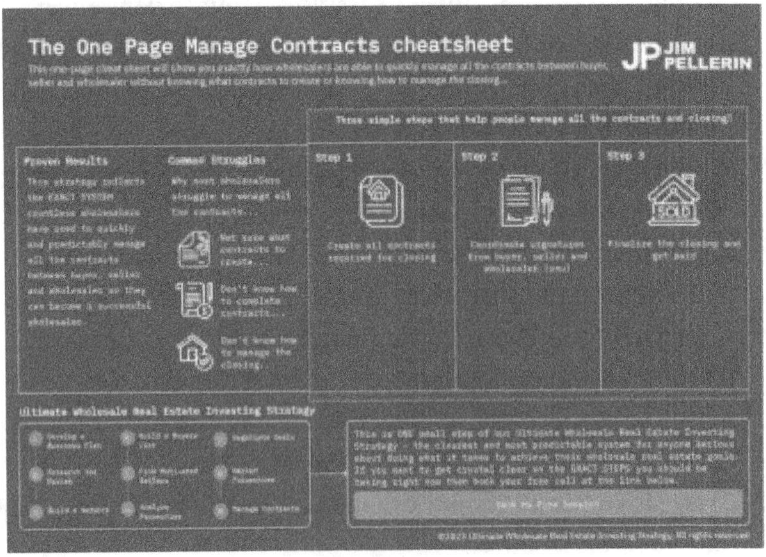

Managing contracts is a crucial step in the wholesale real estate business. It involves handling legal agreements between the buyer, seller, and wholesaler (you). Here are some steps you can take to manage contracts effectively:

1. **Hire a Real Estate Attorney:** A real estate attorney can help you draft and review contracts to ensure they are legally sound. They can also advise you on any potential legal issues and help you navigate complex legal situations.
2. **Use Standardized Contracts:** Use standardized contracts to ensure that all parties involved understand the terms and conditions of the agreement. Standardized contracts are readily available online or through your local real estate association.
3. **Include Contingencies:** Contingencies protect you as the wholesaler in case the deal falls through. Common contingencies include the buyer's ability to secure financing

or the property passing a home inspection.

4. **Understand the Closing Process:** Understanding the closing process is essential for managing contracts. The closing process involves the assignment contract and the transfer of ownership from the seller to the buyer and includes the exchange of funds, payment of fees, and signing of legal documents. Make sure you are familiar with the closing process and can assist your buyer and seller through this process.
5. **Communicate Effectively:** Communicate effectively with all parties involved in the contracts. Ensure that everyone is clear on the terms and conditions of the agreement and keep all parties informed of any updates or changes.
6. **Follow Up:** Follow up with the buyer and seller after the contract is signed to ensure that all parties are meeting their obligations. Follow up on any contingencies and ensure that the closing process is moving forward smoothly.

Managing contracts can be complex, but by hiring a real estate attorney, using standardized contracts, including contingencies, understanding the closing process, communicating effectively, and following up, you can manage contracts effectively and ensure that all parties involved are satisfied with the transaction.

Step 10 - Repeat

The final step in building a successful wholesale real estate business is to repeat the process. The key to success in wholesale real estate is consistency, and you should aim to repeat the steps outlined in this plan consistently to achieve your business goals. Here are some tips to help you repeat the process effectively:

1. **Track Your Results:** Keep track of your results for each deal,

including the time and effort required, the profit margin, and any issues that arose. Use this information to refine your process and make improvements for future deals.

2. **Continuously Learn:** Continuously learn about the market, industry trends, and best practices in wholesale real estate. Attend seminars and conferences, read industry publications, and network with other professionals in the industry.
3. **Refine Your Marketing Strategies:** Continuously refine your marketing strategies to ensure that it is effective in generating leads and finding new buyers and sellers. Test different marketing channels and tactics to see what works best for your business.
4. **Build Your Network:** Continuously build and expand your network of buyers and industry professionals. Attend networking events, join real estate associations, and reach out to potential clients and partners.
5. **Stay Compliant:** Ensure that you are complying with all state and federal regulations for wholesale real estate. Stay up-to-date on changes in regulations and adjust your business practices as needed.

By tracking your results, continuously learning, refining your marketing strategy, building your network, and staying compliant, you can repeat the process of building a successful wholesale real estate business. Remember, consistency is key, and the more deals you complete, the more successful you will become in this industry.

Appendix B: Joint Ventures With Other Wholesalers

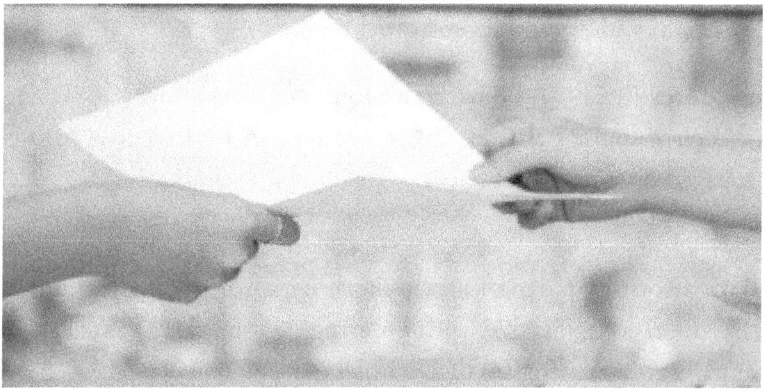

Agreement - Photo by Van Tay Media

Introduction

In today's highly competitive business environment, it is essential for wholesalers to explore innovative strategies to expand their market reach, enhance their product offerings, and increase their profitability. One such strategy is forming **joint ventures with other wholesalers**.

A joint venture is a strategic alliance between two or more wholesalers that agree to pool their resources and expertise to achieve a specific goal.

This section will discuss the benefits of joint ventures, the factors to consider when selecting a joint venture partner, the steps to establish a successful joint venture, and the potential challenges that may arise during the process.

Benefits of Joint Ventures

Access to New Markets: Joint ventures can provide wholesalers with access to new markets and customer segments that they may not have been able to reach on their own. By partnering with a wholesaler that has an established presence in a specific market, a business can quickly gain a foothold and expand its customer base.

Sharing of Resources and Expertise: Joint ventures allow wholesalers to pool their resources and expertise, which can lead to cost savings and improved operational efficiency. This includes marketing and sales efforts.

Risk Mitigation: By partnering with another wholesaler, a wholesaler can share the risks associated with entering new markets. This can be particularly beneficial for smaller wholesalers that may not have the financial resources to expand on their own.

Increased Profitability: By pooling resources, sharing costs, and leveraging each other's strengths, joint ventures can lead to increased profitability for both partners. This can be particularly beneficial in markets with tight profit margins.

Selecting a Joint Venture Partner

Complementary Strengths: When selecting a joint venture partner, it is important to look for wholesalers that have complementary strengths and resources. This can include access to specific markets or focusing on one aspect of wholesaling such as **acquisitions** or **dispositions**.

Shared Vision and Goals: A successful joint venture requires a shared vision and common goals. Before entering into a partnership, it is essential to ensure that both parties have a clear understanding of the objectives of the joint venture and are committed to working together to achieve them.

Financial Stability: It is important to choose a joint venture partner that is financially stable and has the resources to invest in the partnership. This can help to ensure the long-term success of the joint venture and minimize the risk of financial difficulties down the road.

Reputation and Trust: Trust is a critical component of any successful joint venture. It is essential to choose a partner with a strong reputation in the industry and a track record of ethical business practices.

Establishing a Successful Joint Venture

Clear Roles and Responsibilities: To ensure the success of a joint venture, it is important to clearly define the roles and responsibilities of each partner on each deal. This can help to prevent misunderstandings and conflicts down the road.

Legal Structure and Agreements: It is essential to establish a solid legal foundation for the joint venture, including comprehensive joint venture agreements outlining the terms of the partnership for each deal.

Communication and Collaboration: Open and transparent communication is critical to the success of any joint venture. Regular calls and updates can help to ensure that both partners are on the same page and working together effectively.

Performance Metrics and Monitoring: Establishing clear performance metrics and regularly monitoring the progress of the overall joint venture arrangement can help to ensure that both partners are meeting their objectives and that the partnership is on track to achieve its long-term goals.

Challenges of Joint Ventures

Geographical Differences: When partnering with a wholesaler from a different area, it is important to be aware of potential legal differences that may impact the success of the joint venture. This can include differences in ***legal systems***, ***business practices***, and ***expectations***.

Conflicting Interests: In some cases, joint venture partners may have conflicting interests or priorities that can create challenges in the partnership. It is essential to address these issues early on and establish clear guidelines for resolving conflicts.

Loss of Control: By entering into a joint venture, wholesalers may need to relinquish some control over certain aspects of their business. This can be challenging for some wholesalers, particularly if they are used to making all of the decisions themselves.

Conclusion

Joint ventures with other wholesalers can offer significant benefits, including access to new markets, shared resources and expertise, risk mitigation, and increased profitability. However, it is essential to carefully select a joint venture partner, establish a solid legal foundation, and maintain open communication and collaboration throughout!

Check out my website at jimpellerin.com for a free joint venture process map[1].

1. https://jimpellerin.com/wholesale-jv

Appendix C: How to Do a Double Closing

Closing - *Photo by Khwanchai Phanthong*

One important aspect of wholesale real estate transactions is the concept of **double closing** also known as simultaneous closing. It is a process used to complete a wholesale transaction where the wholesaler buys the property from the seller and then immediately resells it to the end buyer. The two transactions take place on the same day, and the wholesaler earns a profit from the difference between the purchase and sale price.

Understanding this process is essential for anyone involved in wholesale real estate transactions. It can be a valuable tool for completing deals quickly and efficiently, but it also involves legal and financial risks that must be carefully managed. By understanding the process and the risks involved, wholesalers can make informed decisions and ensure that they are operating within the bounds of the law. In this section, we will provide a detailed explanation of double closing, including how it works, its benefits and drawbacks, its legality, and when it should be used.

Chapter 1: Introduction to Double Closing

Key Points

- Explanation of what a double closing is and how it differs from an assignment of contract
- Advantages and disadvantages of using a double closing
- Importance of understanding the legal requirements and potential risks involved in a double closing

Introduction

A **double closing**, also known as a **simultaneous closing** or **back-to-back closing**, involves two separate transactions: the first transaction is between the seller and the wholesaler (buyer), while the second transaction is between the wholesaler (seller) and the end buyer. In other words, the wholesaler buys the property from the original seller and then immediately sells it to the end buyer, with the two transactions occurring at the same time.

In contrast, an ***assignment of contract*** involves the wholesaler assigning their contract with the original seller to the end buyer, who then assumes the rights and obligations under that contract. In this case, there is only one transaction between the original seller and the end buyer, with the wholesaler acting as a middleman and receiving an assignment fee.

Advantages of Double Closing

One of the advantages of using a double closing is that it allows wholesalers to **sell properties that they do not own**, thus avoiding any legal issues related to ownership. This method can also allow for more flexibility in terms of financing, as the end buyer is the party that funds the transaction and obtains the financing for the transaction.

Additionally, using a double closing can provide wholesalers with **more control** over the transaction, as they can negotiate the terms of both purchase and sale agreements. This can lead to more favorable terms and higher profits for the wholesaler.

Disadvantages of Double Closing

One of the main disadvantages of using a double closing is that it can be **more complex** and requires more coordination than an assignment of contract. This is because the transaction involves the **two separate closings** and requires the involvement of title companies and other professionals who understand the process.

Another disadvantage of using a double closing is that it can be more expensive due to the **additional closing costs** and fees associated with two separate transactions.

Additionally, the use of a double closing can **attract more scrutiny** from regulatory bodies, as it can be seen as a way to circumvent certain legal requirements.

Legal Requirements and Risks

It is important for wholesalers to understand the legal requirements and potential risks involved in a double closing. Wholesalers **must**

comply with all state and federal laws and regulations related to real estate transactions, including disclosure requirements and anti-fraud laws.

Failure to comply with legal requirements can result in fines and legal action, which can be costly and damaging to a wholesaler's reputation. Additionally, using a double closing can attract more scrutiny from regulatory bodies, making it important for wholesalers to ensure that all aspects of the transaction are conducted in a transparent and ethical manner.

Conclusion

In conclusion, double closing is a useful tool for wholesalers to sell properties without taking ownership. However, it is important for wholesalers to understand the legal requirements and potential risks involved in a double closing. Additionally, wholesalers should carefully consider the advantages and disadvantages of using a double closing versus an assignment of contract, and choose the method that is best suited for their particular situation.

Chapter 2: Legal Requirements for Double Closing

Legal Compliance - Photo by Tingey Injury Law Firm

Key Points

- Overview of legal requirements for double closing, including disclosure and documentation
- Importance of compliance with state and federal laws and regulations
- Discussion of potential consequences of non-compliance, including fines and legal action

Double closing is a legal transaction in wholesale real estate investing, but it is subject to certain legal requirements that must be complied with to avoid potential fines or legal action.

Disclosure Requirements

One of the most important legal requirements for double closing is disclosure. This means that all parties involved in the transaction **must be fully informed** and aware of the nature and terms of the transaction. This includes the ***seller***, the ***buyer***, and any ***other intermediaries*** or stakeholders who may be involved.

For example, the seller must be informed that the wholesaler intends to sell the property to another buyer immediately after closing and that this transaction will involve a double closing. The buyer must also be informed of the double closing, and given the opportunity to review and approve all documentation related to the transaction.

In addition, wholesalers **must comply** with state and federal disclosure requirements, which may vary depending on the jurisdiction and the type of property involved. For example, in some states, wholesalers may be required to provide **additional disclosures** regarding the condition or history of the property, or to comply with specific regulations regarding the use of certain documents or forms.

Documentation Requirements

Another important legal requirement for double closing is documentation. This means that all transactions must be **properly documented**, including ***contracts***, ***agreements***, and any ***other legal or financial documents*** related to the transaction.

For example, the wholesaler must have a contract with the seller that allows them to **market and sell the property** and another contract with the buyer that sets out the **terms of the sale**. These contracts must be properly executed and include all necessary terms and conditions, such as the ***purchase price***, ***closing date***, and any ***contingencies or warranties***.

In addition, wholesalers must comply with state and federal documentation requirements, which may include specific forms or disclosures that must be included in the transaction documents. Failure to comply with these requirements can result in fines or other legal consequences.

Compliance and Consequences

Compliance with legal requirements for double closing is essential to avoid potential **legal and financial consequences**. Failure to comply with these requirements can result in fines, legal action, or other penalties that can have a significant impact on the wholesaler's business.

For example, a wholesaler who **fails to disclose the double closing** to the seller or the buyer may be subject to legal action for fraud or misrepresentation. Similarly, a wholesaler who fails to comply with state or federal documentation requirements may be subject to fines or other penalties for non-compliance.

In addition, non-compliance with legal requirements can damage the wholesaler's reputation and credibility, which can have long-term consequences for their business. By complying with legal requirements for double closing, wholesalers can build a reputation for **professionalism and integrity**, and avoid the potential legal and financial consequences of non-compliance.

Conclusion

In conclusion, compliance with legal requirements for double closing is essential for wholesalers who want to build a successful and sustainable business in wholesale real estate. By understanding the disclosure and documentation requirements, and complying with state and federal laws and regulations, wholesalers can minimize their risks and maximize their profits, while building a reputation for professionalism and integrity.

Chapter 3: Steps Involved in a Double Closing

Process Steps - Photo by geralt

Key Points

- Overview of the steps involved in a double closing, including finding a buyer and coordinating with title companies
- Discussion of common challenges and how to overcome them, such as financing and timing issues
- Importance of communication and collaboration between all parties involved in the transaction

Step 1: Finding a Buyer

The first step in a double closing transaction is finding a buyer who is **willing to purchase the property** from the wholesaler **immediately after the first closing**. The wholesaler may use a variety of strategies to find a buyer, including online marketing, networking, and direct outreach to potential investors.

Once a buyer has been identified, the wholesaler will need to enter into a contract with them that sets out the terms of the sale, including the purchase price, closing date, and any contingencies or warranties.

Step 2: Coordinating with Title Companies

The next step in a double closing transaction is coordinating with title companies to ensure that all **documentation and legal requirements are met**. The wholesaler will need to work closely with the title company to ensure that all contracts and documents are properly executed and recorded, and that all legal requirements are met.

This may involve conducting a title search to identify any liens or encumbrances on the property, obtaining title insurance to protect against any defects or disputes, and coordinating with lenders or other parties to ensure that all financing and funding is in place.

Step 3: Managing Financing and Timing Issues

One of the most common challenges in a double closing transaction is managing financing and timing issues. For example, the wholesaler **may need to secure financing** to purchase the property from the seller, and then quickly resell the property to the buyer at a profit. This can be challenging if there are delays or issues with financing, or if the timing of the transactions is not properly managed.

To overcome these challenges, wholesalers may need to work closely with lenders, investors, and other parties to **ensure that all financing and funding is in place**, and that all transactions are properly coordinated and timed.

Step 4: Communicating and Collaborating with all Parties

Throughout the double closing process, it is essential for wholesalers to **maintain open lines of communication** and collaboration with all parties involved in the transaction. This includes the ***seller***, the ***buyer***, the ***title company***, ***lenders***, and any ***other intermediaries or stakeholders***.

By communicating clearly and proactively, wholesalers can **minimize the risk of misunderstandings or disputes**, and ensure that all parties are fully informed and aware of the nature and terms of the transaction.

Conclusion

In conclusion, the steps involved in a double closing transaction in wholesale real estate can be complex and challenging, but with careful planning, communication, and collaboration, wholesalers can manage the process effectively and achieve their goals.

By finding a buyer, coordinating with title companies, managing financing and timing issues, and communicating with all parties, wholesalers can minimize risks and maximize profits, while building a reputation for professionalism and integrity.

Chapter 4: Summary of Tips for a Successful Double Closing

Tips - Photo by Sam Dan Truong

Key Points

- Strategies for mitigating risks and avoiding potential pitfalls in a double closing
- Tips for negotiating favorable terms and maximizing profits
- Discussion of best practices for managing and executing a double closing

Whiles most of these tips have already been mentioned in previous sections, it's importance to remphasize them here to ensure a success double-closing.

Tip 1: Understand and Comply with Legal Requirements

To avoid legal issues and potential penalties, it is important to understand and comply with all legal requirements for double closing transactions. This includes disclosing all relevant information to all parties involved, obtaining all necessary documentation, and following state and federal regulations. Wholesalers should work closely with legal and financial professionals to ensure that they are fully compliant with all legal requirements and regulations.

Tip 2: Establish Clear Communication and Collaboration with all Parties Involved

Effective communication and collaboration between all parties involved in the transaction is crucial for success in a double closing. This includes maintaining clear and open lines of communication with the seller, the buyer, the title company, lenders, and any other intermediaries or stakeholders. Wholesalers should ensure that all parties are informed and aware of the nature and terms of the transaction, and that all questions and concerns are addressed promptly.

Tip 3: Negotiate Favorable Terms for the Double Closing

To maximize profits in a double closing transaction, it is important to negotiate favorable terms for both the purchase and sale agreements. This includes negotiating a favorable purchase price with the seller, as well as a favorable sale price with the buyer. Wholesalers should also consider negotiating other terms, such as the timing of the transaction and any contingencies or warranties.

Tip 4: Manage Financing and Timing Issues Carefully

Financing and timing issues can be major challenges in a double closing transaction, and it is important to manage them carefully. This may involve securing financing in advance, coordinating with lenders or investors, and managing the timing of the transactions to ensure that all parties are able to meet their obligations. Wholesalers should also be prepared to address any unexpected delays or issues that may arise during the process.

Tip 5: Execute the Double Closing Efficiently

Efficient execution of the double closing is critical for success. This includes ensuring that all contracts and documents are properly executed and recorded, and that all legal requirements and regulations are met. Wholesalers should work closely with the title company to ensure that all paperwork and documentation is in order, and that all parties are prepared for the closing.

Conclusion

In conclusion, executing a successful double closing transaction in wholesale real estate requires careful planning, effective communication, and close collaboration between all parties involved. By understanding and complying with legal requirements, negotiating favorable terms, managing financing and timing issues, and executing the double closing efficiently, wholesalers can minimize risks, maximize profits, and build a reputation for professionalism and integrity.

Chapter 5: Case Studies Examples

Case Study - Photo by Pixabay

Key Points

- Analysis of real-life examples of successful and unsuccessful double closings
- Discussion of lessons learned and best practices for future transactions
- Importance of continual learning and adapting to changing market conditions and regulations.

Case Study 1: Successful Double Closing

A wholesaler, let's call him John, identified a distressed property with a motivated seller. John negotiated a favorable purchase price with the seller and then found a buyer who was interested in purchasing the property for a higher price. John then arranged for a double closing, where he bought the property from the seller and immediately sold it to the buyer. The transaction was completed without any issues, and John made a profit of $20,000.

Lessons Learned

- Effective negotiation skills are key to securing favorable purchase and sale prices.
- Identifying motivated sellers and finding the right buyer are crucial steps in a successful double closing.
- Proper planning and coordination with all parties involved are necessary to execute the transaction smoothly.

Case Study 2: Unsuccessful Double Closing

Another wholesaler, let's call him David, found a property that he wanted to wholesale. David signed a contract with the seller and then found a buyer who was willing to purchase the property for a higher price. However, David did not properly disclose to the buyer that he was purchasing the property from the seller and reselling it to them, resulting in confusion and mistrust from the buyer. The transaction ultimately fell apart, and David was unable to complete the double closing.

Lessons Learned

- Proper disclosure and transparency are crucial in a double closing transaction.
- Failure to disclose relevant information can result in mistrust and ultimately, the failure of the transaction.
- Communication and collaboration with all parties involved are important to ensure that all parties are aware of the nature and terms of the transaction.

Best Practices

Based on the above case studies, we can draw some **best practices** for executing successful double closing transactions in wholesale real estate. These include:

- Understanding and complying with all legal requirements and regulations.
- Identifying motivated sellers and finding the right buyer.
- Negotiating favorable terms for both the purchase and sale agreements.
- Properly disclosing all relevant information to all parties involved.
- Coordinating financing and timing issues carefully.
- Efficient execution of the double closing.

Importance of Continual Learning

Finally, it is important for wholesalers to continually learn and adapt to changing market conditions and regulations. This can involve attending industry events, staying up-to-date with legal and regulatory developments, and networking with other professionals in the industry. By staying informed and adapting to changing conditions, wholesalers can increase their chances of success and build a reputation for professionalism and expertise in the industry.

About The Author

JIM PELLERIN started real estate investing over twenty years ago. Since then, he has bought and sold millions of dollars of real estate. He began by purchasing and renting out duplexes. Following that he added Lease Options to his strategy. He has implemented many creative funding strategies that have allowed him to continue implementing various strategies and alloqed him to build a sizable portfolio.

As part of his education, he has attended numerous seminars on real estate investing, project management, property management, financing, renovations, motivation, time management, and many more. He has also read over 500 books on similar topics.

This book blends his experience and the knowledge he has gained through his investments and studies.

Visit his author page to discover my other publications: books2read.com/JimPellerin[1]

1. https://books2read.com/JimPellerin

Other Books By Jim Pellerin

Real Estate Investing: Strategies – The Secret to Financial Independence with Real Estate

books2read.com/strategies[1]

1. https://books2read.com/strategies

Real Estate Investing with Lease Options – How to Invest with No Money Down

books2read.com/Lease-Options[2]

2. https://books2read.com/Lease-Options

Invest NOW – The Passive Approach to Winning with Real Estate

books2read.com/investnow[3]

3. https://books2read.com/investnow

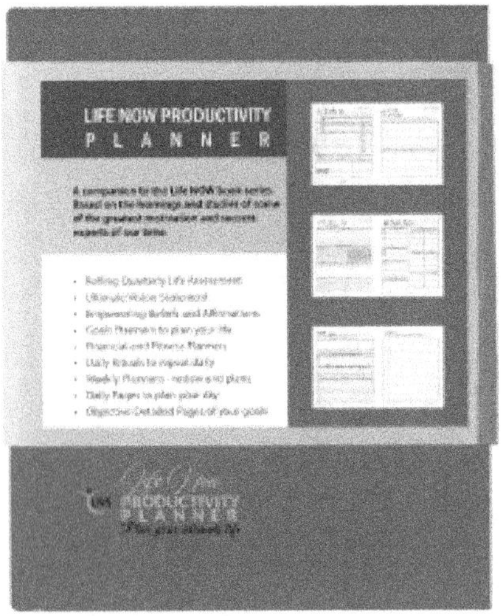

books2read.com/JimPellerin[4]

4. https://books2read.com/JimPellerin

Don't miss out!

Visit the website below and you can sign up to receive emails whenever Jim Pellerin publishes a new book. There's no charge and no obligation.

https://books2read.com/r/B-A-WGIX-EEMIC

Did you love *The Ultimate Beginners Guide to Wholesale Real Estate Investing*? Then you should read *Real Estate Investing Strategies: The Secret to Financial Independence with Real Estate*[5] by Jim Pellerin!

[6]

The mechanics of Real Estate Investing is simple: Buy a house and do something with it. Fix it and rent it, or just sell it. Sounds simple, doesn't it? Yet only a small percentage of us have enough courage to go out and take advantage of the opportunities that are available to us. Real Estate Investing can be more promising than stocks, bonds, and various other securities because of the higher rates of return.

In this book, I show you how to get started by describing the different types of skills you need, by showing you how to take control of your personal and financial situation, and by helping you decide what type of real estate investing you want to get involved in. I also show

5. https://books2read.com/u/m2QyNG

6. https://books2read.com/u/m2QyNG

you how to find properties, how to analyze them, and how to make an offer that makes sense. And finally, I describe what you need to do to manage your investment and ultimately how to sell your investment for the most profit.

I have been involved in real estate investing for over 20 years. I have yet to find a book that focuses on the investor and the overall process. Sure, there are lots of books on fix and flips, buy, rent and hold, rent to own, etc. However, I haven't found any good books on how to really get started in the real estate investing process from a practical viewpoint. The technical aspects of real estate investing are really quite easy. But if it's so easy, then why isn't everyone doing it?

This book is for people who are serious about getting started in real estate investing and who want to join the 5% of those who actually take action and invest. This book provides a strategic approach with the tried and tested methods and principles that have helped others make millions in real estate.

Read more at www.jimpellerin.com.

Also by Jim Pellerin

Real Estate Investing

Real Estate Investing Strategies: The Secret to Financial Independence with Real Estate

Real Estate Investing with Lease Options - Investing in Real Estate with No Money Down

Invest Now - The Passive Approach to Winning at Real Estate

The Ultimate Beginners Guide to Real Estate Investing

The 98 Best Real Estate Investing Strategies

The Ultimate Beginners Guide to Wholesale Real Estate Investing

Watch for more at www.jimpellerin.com.

www.ingramcontent.com/pod-product-compliance
Lightning Source LLC
LaVergne TN
LVHW022042200926
848481LV00003B/751
* 9 7 9 8 2 2 3 9 4 1 0 1 9 *